VIBRANT
PUBLISHERS

D0080381

SAT ESSAY WRITING:

GUIDE WITH SAMPLE PROMPTS

Fourth Edition

◆ **16 sample prompts**

◆ **Passages from high-quality published sources**

◆ **Pre-writing guidance**

◆ **Sample essay responses**

SAT Essay Writing
Guide with Sample Prompts

ISBN-10: 1-949395-62-6
ISBN-13: 978-1-949395-62-4
Library of Congress Control Number: 2018903988

Vibrant Publishers books are available at special quantity discount for sales promotions, or for use in corporate training programs. For more information please write to bulkorders@vibrantpublishers.com

Please email feedback / corrections (technical, grammatical or spelling) to spellerrors@vibrantpublishers.com

To access the complete catalogue of Vibrant Publishers, visit www.vibrantpublishers.com

Table of Contents

1   SAT Overview   **5**

What is the SAT   6

Preparing for the SAT   6

Words to Know   7

Who takes the SAT   8

Who administers the SAT   8

What is tested?   9

Scoring   11

2   The SAT Essay: Introduction   **13**

Essay Overview   14

Why the Essay Matters   14

Essay Prompt   15

Getting Started on the Essay   16

Scoring   17

Strategies for writing an effective essay   19

Vocabulary   24

Literary devices to use for writing a good essay   26

Practice and Plan   27

3   Solved Essays   **29**

Essay 1-   31

Essay 2-   39

Essay 3-   49

Essay 4-   58

Essay 5-   67

Essay 6-   75

Essay 7-   83

Essay 8-   92

Essay 9- 100

Essay 10- 110

Essay 11- 118

Essay 12- 126

Essay 13- 135

Essay 14- 143

Essay 15- 151

Essay 16- 159

Dear Student,

Thank you for purchasing **SAT Essay Writing Guide with Sample Prompts.** We are committed to publishing books that are content-rich, concise and approachable enabling more students to read and make the fullest use of them. We hope this book provides the most enriching learning experience as you prepare for your SAT exam.

Should you have any questions or suggestions, feel free to email us at reachus@vibrantpublishers.com

Thanks again for your purchase. Good luck for your SAT!

– Vibrant Publishers Team

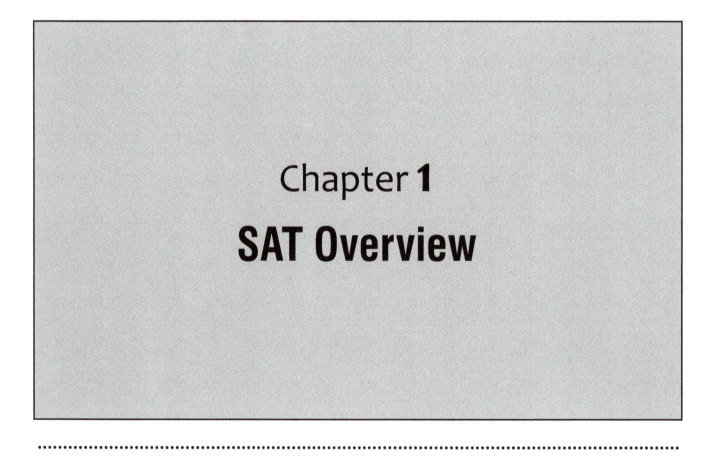

Chapter **1**

SAT Overview

So, you've decided to take the SAT. At this point in your life you probably have a lot of important decisions looming in front of you. What college would I like to attend? What do I need to get in? What classes should I be taking? What's a good GPA? Of course, you are also wondering about the SAT. This chapter provides an overview of the SAT as one of the data points considered for college entrance standards. It also provides the outline of the test, grading overview and some helpful hints to get you started. The most important first step is to know what to expect, so you can make the best-informed choices as you look forward to your exciting future. Congratulations on taking that first step.

What is the SAT?

The SAT (Standardized Aptitude Test) is one of the two primary tests which colleges use to gauge whether or not you might be ready for college. It is a test that reflects the things you should have learned in high school and relies on strategic questioning to actively represent those skills and knowledge that are essential as you enter the world of college. But what is it really? The SAT is a measure of how well you can take what you learned and apply it to a timed testing environment. It shows how well you take tests and how well you do in a stressful situation. It does not however, measure your intelligence. In fact, once you learn the tips and tricks of the test, one might argue it measures your testing ability more than what you know.

If that's what it is, why do colleges use it for a standard for admission? Colleges use this as a predictive analytic tool to try to figure out if you have the basic abilities required of a college freshman. They want to make sure you can comprehend reading at a level that is expected in your classes. Same with math: do you have a basic understanding of mathematical concepts, so you can succeed not just in math class but in other required classes such as economics. Many colleges also want to see if you can write in a way that is conducive to the college classroom. Again, they are not testing whether or not you CAN write but whether or not you can follow instructions and apply what you read to create an essay that would be appropriate for the college classroom. Finally, they are assessing your ability to take lengthy, timed tests. This testing situation mirrors what you might encounter in your college classes. They want to make sure, when they check that box for YES, they will be admitting someone with the tools to succeed. Colleges and universities must report their success rates with students and if all their students drop out, because they are not prepared to succeed, then the college itself cannot succeed. That is one reason why the admission process is so rigorous.

Preparing for the SAT

Knowing all that, it is essential to understand the tips and tricks of this assessment. The SAT is a great vehicle to show what you know. It has recently been realigned with the current high school college readiness curriculum, so it does reflect what you have seen in your classroom. But like any other test, it requires preparation and planning to do your best. It is important to note that you can take the test more than once. It won't count against you to try again, and in the end, you can choose the test you would like to send. Some schools super score, which means you can combine the best sections into one final score. (You can read more about that in the "Words to Know" section). All these options are handy, especially if test taking isn't one of your strengths, but the real goal should be to go into your first testing situation with a plan to succeed. Here are some tips to prepare for that first testing day:

a) Learn strategies, tips and tools

b) Practice, practice, practice. The more questions you see; the better you will do

c) Learn math and reading formulas

d) Practice the essay

e) Create a study group and learn from your friends

You also need to:

a) Understand the purpose of the test

b) Outline the standards and requirements of each section

c) Learn strategies and practices that will help you do your best on the test

d) And above all, know what to expect and develop a plan to succeed

On the day of the test he re are some things to remember:

a) Get a good night's sleep and relax. Remember it is not the end of the world if you don't have your best testing day. You can always take the test again.

b) Gather your testing supplies. Take several sharpened number 2 pencils, pencil you feel comfortable writing with, if you are taking the essay section, and your calculator (make sure it follows the guidelines set forth by the College Board).

c) It is always smart to take a snack with you for your breaks. This will help energize you and keep you going.

d) Don't forget your picture ID and your testing ticket. Make sure to double check all the requirements on the College Board site. They will give you a detailed account of all the documents you need to bring.

Words to Know

❑ **College Board:** The College Board is the manager of the SAT. This organization provides great resources to better understand the application process, the meaning of your score, and the components of the test.

❑ **Standardized:** Standardized means the same for all. Everyone taking the SAT will be tested on standardized material. There is no truth in the old myth that a red cover is a harder version, or if you take the test in June, it's easier than if you take it in January. Whenever you take it, regardless of the color of your test, the content is the same.

- ❑ **ACT:** This is a test similar to the SAT. When the SAT was redesigned, it became more aligned with the content of the ACT. Now the two tests are pretty similar. Both tests are equally important, and you should consult your colleges of choice to see which they prefer.

- ❑ **Data Point:** You might hear the SAT mentioned as a data point. This means it is just one measure, one point of data that is used to predict whether or not you will be a good fit for the college or university. Remember, they are using a predicative analysis formula to find the best fit for their programs and campus mission. You'll notice that every institution rates data points differently so that those skills they value most will be the biggest data points to consider.

- ❑ **Old SAT vs. New SAT:** In 2016, the SAT made some major changes to its format, grading formula and essay. For the first year that these changes were in place, students could choose which format they would like to take. However, now there is just one SAT. When you sit for the exam, you can be assured that everyone else sitting for the exam that day is receiving a similar version of the test.

- ❑ **Super score:** A Super score is when after taking the SAT multiple times, you combine the best scores for each section to create the Super score that you send to your school. For example, if you rocked the first math test but just bombed the reading, if you chose to take it again, and did great on the reading, your score could be composed of the math from the first test and the reading from the second. This sounds great, right? However, this is not a College Board thing. This is a school to school decision. You need to check with the schools you intend to apply to and see if they Super score. If they do not, then you will use the total scores from each individual test. This is an important distinction.

Who takes the SAT?

The typical test taker is a student planning to enter a undergraduate program in the United States or Canada. The SAT may be a requirement for admission, but it is important to check with your colleges of choice to see if they prefer the SAT or ACT. It is also essential to see if they require the essay. Typically, this test is taken in the 11th and 12th grade.

Who administers the SAT?

On the day of the test, your exam will be administered by trained proctors. They are employees of the College Board and they specialize in test security. They are not able to answer questions about the test but can answer your logistical questions such as where to take a break and when the test starts. They read their instructions from a script, so the College Board can ensure that every test taker is receiving the same information. They are also responsible for watching for testing anomalies or misadministration issues.

The SAT is administered by the College Board. The College Board is an organization which writes, evaluates and manages the registration for the exam. They are your one stop shop for anything you need to know about actually taking the test. You can register through their site as well as receive your final score. Once you register and choose your schools, the College Board will also send your scores directly to your schools of choice. They also provide a thorough explanation of your scores, so you can see your highs and lows and make plans for improvements, if you are considering retaking the test.

Remember, even though you may take the test at your high school, it is not your school that is responsible for the test. The College Board creates, grades and secures all tests, so they can ensure test security. In other words, they can guarantee that you took the correct test with the correct results.

What is tested?

The SAT is divided into four sections:

a) Essay

b) Reading

c) Writing and language

d) Math

Essay

The essay is an optional section on the test. However, it is recommended that unless you know for sure that your school doesn't consider the essay, you should take it. Remember, if you have to go back to take the test, you can't just take the essay section. You have to take the whole thing again!

The essay section begins with a passage. You read the passage and then create a response that discusses the argumentative elements in the passage and how successful the author was in delivering the main idea of the piece. You should also be able to discuss that main idea and the supporting details found throughout the essay. Word choice, sentence structure and general comprehension are all important components of this section.

Remember, this doesn't measure you as a writer. It measures your understanding and ability to comprehend the task, the passage and put it together into a well packaged piece.

You have 50 minutes to complete this task and it is graded on reading, analysis and writing. Each one of these grading points receives a score from 2-8, which gives you an overall score between 6 and 24. Keep in mind that this is a written assignment so make sure to bring pencils or pens you feel comfortable using.

Reading

The Reading test consists of 52 multiple choice questions and you have 65 minutes to complete it. You'll encounter passages or pairs of passages that are considered literature, historical documents, social sciences and natural sciences. The biggest advantage you have in this test is to choose the order you attack the passages. The best strategy is to practice. Your strategy will improve as you begin to understand your strengths and opportunities. That understanding comes with practice. For example, if you are a wiz at the historical document, you might want to do that one first and get it out of the way, so you can focus on the natural science passage that you know is a passage that will require more of your time.

You can also learn about question types and develop strategies for each one. The question types you will see include;

a) Main idea/big picture questions

b) Detail questions

c) Inference questions

d) Author's purpose and technique questions

e) Vocabulary questions

f) Analogy questions

g) Data reasoning

h) Use of evidence support

Each question type carries with it its own strategies and tips. The first step is to be able to decide which question type you are encountering. After you know what type of the question it is, you can decide first what kind of answer you are looking for and next how to use the passage to find the answer. However, as you are deciding these strategies, the clock is ticking, which is why practicing is essential.

Here are some quick tips to get you started:

a) Know what to expect: format, time, expectations.

b) Choose the order of passages.

c) Read the passages in a way that makes sense to answer the questions. You don't have to necessarily read every word to answer these questions.

d) Remember this is a passage-based assessment. They are not looking for what you think or what you know. Focus on what the passage says. That's all that matters.

e) Save main idea questions for the last. By that time, you will have lived with the passage long enough to get the gist of what it is saying.

Writing and Language

You will have 35 minutes for the 44 multiple choice questions in this section. Questions cover grammar, vocabulary and editing. You will start with four passages and work through the questions in context. What this means is that every question offers you a chance to practice real skills such as editing, choosing the best word and re-ordering sentences. You will be also asked several reading comprehension questions mostly relating to topic sentences and details. Don't get too caught up in reading the passages but make sure as you are working through the questions, you have a general idea of what is going on in the passage. That makes it much easier to answer those tricky reading comprehension questions. You also may need to interpret graphics so make sure you understand their role in the overall passage.

Math

The math section is divided into two parts with a total of 58 questions. Note that in the first section, you cannot use your calculator for the 20 questions. This section takes 25 minutes. The second section has 38 questions and lasts for 55 minutes. In this part, you can use your calculator.

The match section covers four main topics.

a) Heart of Algebra

b) Problem Solving and Data Analysis

c) Passport to Advanced Math

d) Additional Topics in Math

The most important thing in this section is to know what the question is asking. Make sure you have worked through all the steps to reach the answer the test really wants. Often times, not completing that last step or not converting inches to feet or pounds to ounces is the difference between a correct and incorrect answer. Also read the word problems carefully. Use your reading strategies to find keywords and again, make sure you understand what they want to see. Finally make sure you are able to use and apply the basic math formulas required for this test. The College Board website provides a comprehensive list of those formulas. Knowing what formula goes with what problem is a big first step towards math success.

Scoring

The SAT has two main scores: Evidence-based Reading and Writing and Math.

For each section you can score between 200 and 800 points. A perfect final score is 1600. Here are some terms to better understand your score. Your total score is the sum of the Reading and Writing and Math sections. This can range between 400 and 1600. A section score is the score you receive on each of the separate sections: Reading and Writing and Math. Remember Reading and Writing are scored as one section. This can be helpful to students who have strengths in one of the sections but struggle in the other. They will eventually balance each other. A percentile is the comparison between you and the rest of the students who took the SAT in the year of your test. This is a test that 11th and 12th graders can take, so you will be compared with all students, not just those students in your grade. A cross-test score shows how you performed on select questions that represent knowledge in science and history. Finally, a subs core is reported as a number between 1-15 and it shows how you perform on basic knowledge questions that specifically relate to what you learned in high school. Topics include: a) Command of Evidence, b) Words in Context, c) Expression of Ideas and d) Standard English Conventions for Reading and Writing and Language tests and a) Heart of Algebra, b) Problem Solving and Data Analysis and c) Passport to Advanced Math for Math test.

The calculation of your overall score is a bit tricky. First there is a raw score. A raw score is found through how many questions you got right. You are not penalized for skipping or guessing questions, but you should always attack each question with your best strategies. Then your score is "equated." What this means is basically your score is curved. The way the curve is determined is far more complicated than you need to understand to figure out your score, but here is the gist. The College Board takes all the tests and determines a high and low scoring range. Based on those highs and lows they set their scale. This scale tries to smooth out all the different testing situations, so everyone's curve is pretty much the same. The bottom line is that the curve never really makes that much difference in your final score. If you have a high raw score, you will have a high SAT score. So, the best strategy is to get as many right answers as you can.

Remember the essay is scored separately. If you take it, you will get a score between 6 and 24. This section is scored by real graders who are highly trained in reading and assessing this writing. Just like with the test, the best strategy is to practice and hit as many required points as possible. The graders work with a rubric and this will help you land a higher score.

Now that you know the basics you are ready to get started. The key is to practice and know what to expect. Good luck and get practicing.

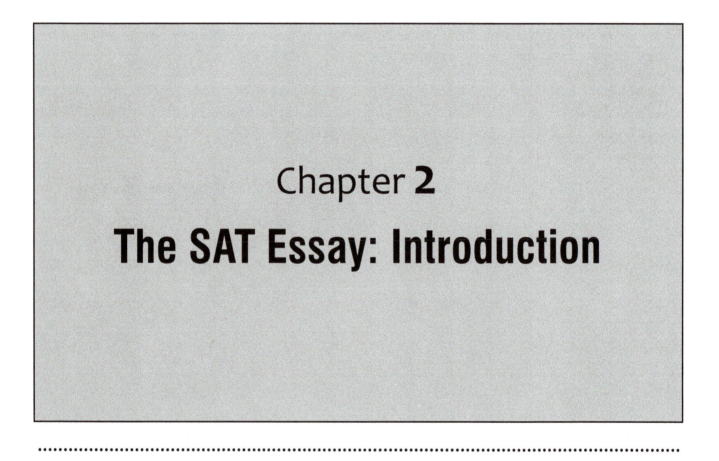

Chapter 2
The SAT Essay: Introduction

Essay Overview

The SAT is a tool that helps colleges and universities better understand your skills and knowledge to predict whether they will fit in with the expectations of their academic programs. It is one data point that is used in a holistic analysis to understand who you are as a student. The SAT Essay is an optional section of the test. In 2016, the SAT underwent several format and function changes. One of the changes was to align the essay task with the ACT by changing its status to optional. Additionally, the score of the essay is no longer calculated as a part of the writing and language score. While the total score of the SAT can measure up to 1600, the 24 points you can receive on the essay, now act as a separate calculation and don't add into your total score. The essay section assesses your reading comprehension and writing skills. It also measures your ability to analytically think as you work through the essay task. The task analyses your reading, analysis and writing abilities with three distinct scores. Each score is outlined through a rubric provided to the highly trained scorers.

Not only was the essay status and scoring changed, but its content also received a facelift. Before the 2016 change, the essay section was much different. There was a heavier emphasis on the writing portion of the task and the ability of the student to craft an opinionated piece, focusing on a provided prompt. This essay task was changed because it did not embody the real tasks that are representative of expected college-level work. The new essay format allows students to demonstrate skills that are much better aligned with not only what you will be expected to do in college, but also with what you were taught in high school. Remember, the point of the SAT is to offer a predictive analysis of your skills and knowledge to ensure that you can be successful in the college environment.

Why the Essay Matters?

Now that the essay is optional, there is a definite debate regarding why it might be a good decision to take it. The first step is to look at the colleges you are considering and ask about their essay policy. If you are absolutely sure their policies won't change, and you are absolutely sure that you won't be considering any other schools, then perhaps you might choose not to take it. But remember, if there are any last-minute changes, it means that you might have to take the entire SAT again. If your school doesn't Super score, it may also mean taking a lower score overall just so that your score includes the essay.

Here are some other reasons to take the essay section:

a) By taking the essay, you have ensured that any last-minute decisions are already covered. Once you sit for the SAT, it's daunting to go back. Even though it does add time to your test, it makes sure you are covered for any situation that might later arise.

b) The cost makes sense. To take the essay with your SAT, it is only an additional eleven dollars. If you have to retake the whole thing it costs over $50. From a cost perspective, it just makes sense to take it all together.

c) Sometimes when you are applying to college, every bit matters. Even if a college doesn't require the SAT essay, showing them that you not only took it, but you did a great job may give you a bit of a boost. Especially if you consider yourself a good writer, it really can't hurt. Also, it can't hurt your overall score. That provides another reason to check it out and take a chance.

d) The breakdown of the score, offers you a picture of what you did well and those areas that might need more practice. It's a great way to get feedback on your writing before writing for the college environment. Writing for your college professors is a completely new thing from what you have been doing in high school. Understanding your strengths and weaknesses through this writing is a good place to start before you are faced with doing it for real.

Essay Prompt

Your journey through the essay begins with a prompt. Even though they are fairly standardized, it is essential to understand each component of the task. Here is the text of the writing prompt that comes with the reading passage:

As you read the passage below, consider how [the author] uses

- ❑ *evidence, such as facts or examples, to support claims.*

- ❑ *reasoning to develop ideas and to connect claims and evidence.*

- ❑ *stylistic or persuasive elements, such as word choice or appeals to emotion, to add power to the ideas expressed.*

<Reading Passage>

Write an essay in which you explain how [the author] builds an argument to persuade [his/her] audience that [author's claim]. In your essay, analyze how [the author] uses one or more of the features listed above (or features of your own choice) to strengthen the logic and persuasiveness of [his/her] argument. Be sure that your analysis focuses on the most relevant features of the passage.

Your essay should not explain whether you agree with [the author's] claims, but rather explain how the author builds an argument to persuade [his/her] audience.

Let's take it apart and consider the different elements you can choose to include:

a) Consider how the author uses evidence. You want to look for facts, statistics or quotes.

b) Analyze how the author uses reasoning devices to connect claims and evidence. You will want to connect your writing through the author's use of ethos, pathos and or logos. The best essays show how each of these are used to strengthen the overall work.

c) Think through how the author uses stylistic elements such as choice of words, appeal to emotions or power of ideas. Look for the use of literary devices such as humor, repetition, analogies or metaphors. Focus on the basic craft of writing.

Getting Started on the Essay

The new essay can be divided between the following three tasks:

a) **Reading:** Reading and comprehending the main idea of the text

b) **Analysis:** Explaining how the author used argumentative elements within the passage to craft his/her writing. Supporting your argument with evidence from the text

c) **Writing:** Writing your response in a concise and comprehensive method that reflects the abilities and vocabulary of a college-ready student

The first step of the essay task is to read the provided passage and prompt and demonstrate your understanding of the main idea, supporting details and elements of author's argument. You want to craft an understanding of how all these elements work together to form a cohesive idea. You also want to understand how the piece is organized and how it works as an overall passage.

The next step is analysis. Your explanation should include your analysis of the author's use of argumentative details in the passage. It should also reflect the understanding of literary devices and their application within an argument. These concepts include main ideas, details, text organization and author's purpose. You might also reference tools of logic such as pathos, logos and ethos. Be aware of the author's use of language and evidence to define stylistic elements. These components will help you weave the story of the passage into a compelling analysis of the author's work.

Once you get your ideas together, think about the craft of writing and your use of language. It is very important that you choose words which fit your task. Just using advanced vocabulary is not enough to score well. You need to learn to use the words purposefully and correctly. You also need to vary sentence structure, use proper sentence construction and develop a logical argumentative flow.

The biggest challenge of the essay section is the timing. You have 50 minutes to read, write and edit your work. To be fair, that is 25 more minutes than the old essay where you were only required to write about a provided topic. Often, it is the reading which throws off the timing of even the most prepared student. That is why practicing not only the reading and the writing, but also practicing the timing is essential. You need to understand how you should divide your time to read, write and edit the work. It is important that you work toward creating a finished essay, complete with an introduction and conclusion. The essay scorers want to see a completed, well-formed and properly supported argument.

Scoring

The SAT essay is scored by trained professionals. Two scorers analyze your essay and each awards one to four points for all three sections: reading, analysis and writing. The two scores are added up and this constitutes your final score for each section. Your total score for each section will be between 2 and 8. Scores of all the three sections are added to get your final score ranging between 6 and 24. The scorers score using a specific rubric that highlights requirements for each section.

Reading

The following should be avoided to make sure you don't score low in this section. Including no information about the main idea or supporting details. The essays may focus too heavily on a discussion of the argument or perhaps they don't discuss much of anything at all. To score low in this section you really have to ignore the topic. This happens when you don't take the time to understand the main idea of the essay and just search for the argumentative elements. It also happens when you don't understand the task itself and write instead about your opinions or address an unrelated topic.

To get a good score, focus on the following:

a) The essay should show comprehension of the text and its ideas.

b) You should address the main idea and use well-supported evidence to explain the details which support it.

The top scoring essays in the reading section demonstrate the following components:

a) An understanding of the story told through a main focus and its supporting details. These essays provide an account of the interrelation of the components and show a real understanding of what, why and how the text is put together.

b) There are no errors in understanding. Not only do these essays explain the main idea and details, they do it according to the information presented in the text. There are no outside ideas brought in to support it, and the information that is presented is done so correctly.

Analysis

The analysis section requires an analysis of how the author uses evidence, stylistic devices and reasoning in building his/her argument. Make sure you carefully explain your main points in a very clear manner. Label your evidence and walk the scorer through your thought process. When you read over your work, there should be a unified account of how the argument was supported and why it was successful.

Avoid ambiguity and support the author's claims with evidence. Remember, it is not enough to say that author makes a good argument. Make sure you are naming the literary devices used in the passage etc explain the elements and analysis of the argument.

To develop a top scoring essay, consider these tips:

a) The essay should focus on the interrelation of the arguments presented and the evidences that support them.

b) You can discuss evidence, reasoning and or stylist elements that the author has chosen to further the purpose of the piece. You show not only what was chosen to support the argument, but also explain why it matters and why it was chosen. Remember, it's not enough just to list the evidence. You also need to discuss why it matters.

c) You focus on those parts of the text which are important to your purpose. Please don't think that you need to list every single device that you find in the passage. You need to strategically choose the rhetorical devices that best support your core argument.

Writing

The writing section is all about language. A score which is not adequate is given when the basic conventions of writing and grammar are not present. Things such as punctuation, capitalization errors, spelling mistakes and misuse of words can impact your score. Make sure you know basic grammar rules such as subject-verb agreement and parallel writing. It is also important to be cognizant of words with multiple meanings. For example, silly errors using to or two or too can point to an issue with the language and can lower your score. Using big words incorrectly is another red flag in this section.

A good score contains writing with few understandable errors. The piece is organized through paragraphs with an introductory and conclusion sentence in each. The sentences themselves vary in length and most of your words are spelled correctly. You have probably included advanced vocabulary here as well.

The exceptional scores are given when the pieces are organized through a skillful introduction and conclusion outlining main points, highlighting central arguments and organizing thoughts through a roadmap. There is a progression of ideas and there is a wide variety of sentence structures. Advanced language is used to build your story rather than put in as an extra device. Generally, there are no overt errors. Overall, there is a tone to these essays that appeals to the reader, shows personality and expresses an understanding of the task and of writing itself.

Strategies for writing an effective essay

Let's practice some of the most successful strategies. Here is the passage we will be referencing.

As you read the passage below, consider how Erin Donovan uses

- ❑ evidence, such as facts or examples, to support claims.

- ❑ reasoning to develop ideas and to connect claims and evidence.

- ❑ stylistic or persuasive elements, such as word choice or appeals to emotion, to add power to the ideas expressed.

Saving for Life. Adapted from Erin Donovan, "Saving your future" 2017

1. Sometimes saving for retirement seems overwhelming. When trying to make ends meet, retirement is often the last thing on a long list of priorities. The promise of starting tomorrow is often the thing that keeps retirement savings from becoming a line on the budget. However, as the years pass, retirement savings must become a focus. It is my suggestion to save small to get big results. Salary savings, smart budgeting and proper support are all ways to make savings happen and allow a financed retirement to become a possibility for even the tightest budget.

2. One place to start is dedicating a small amount from your paycheck each month to retirement savings. The trick is never sacrificing that amount, even for an emergency. Though it seems like a drop of rain in the ocean, raising that amount by one percent a year will lead to big differences in the end. The key to making that financial transformation is a dedicated savings plan, to ensure that you continue to pursue your end results. Really, the idea is to take a long view. Don't be frustrated by seeing a marginal difference in your savings from month to month. Instead, look at the year-to-year comparison to see the difference your dedicated savings is making to your retirement's bottom line. Small savings and incrementally increasing year to year is then the first place to start.

3. The next step is to challenge your spending. Taking a realistic view of your expenses and finding even the smallest savings can affect your bottom line and the amount you have to save. Consider this experiment: write out your budget. Now test each item and ask, "Do I really need this?" Of course, there are items such as bills and mortgage payments that can't be forgone, but even cancelling one night out is a wise place to start. If you are looking for a one percent increase, saying no to a hundred-dollar dinner might achieve just that. Again, you must take the long view, knowing that for every dinner you abandon now, you may be afforded weeks or even months of retirement in the future. This is one of the easiest ways to save for those of us on tight budgets.

4. Don't forget to look for help. Find out what matching programs your employer offers. Do they offer any financial counseling or advising programs? Maybe there are free webinars you can attend online. Regard

less of where you find help, a key to a successful savings plan is to have another set of eyes looking at your budget. A financial advisor knows the rules and ropes of the retirement industry and can point you towards real savings. That is advice worth paying for.

5. So, with the help of an expert, a close look at your budget and a long view of a savings plan, you can really succeed in creating a sustainable retirement plan. It may just take small steps along the way to get there, but following this advice, you'll make it.

•••

Write an essay in which you explain how the author builds an argument to persuade her audience that saving for retirement is possible. In your essay, analyze how the author uses one or more of the features listed above (or features of your own choice) to strengthen the logic and persuasiveness of her argument. Be sure that your analysis focuses on the most relevant features of the passage.

Your essay should not explain whether you agree with the author's claims, but rather explain how the author builds an argument to persuade the audience.

•••

Keeping Active

As you read, you should employ active reading strategies. Active reading is working through a piece by utilizing skills that move you beyond just reading words. Some of these skills include underlining, chunking text passages, labeling ideas and outlining the argumentative components of the piece. This makes it much easier to use each one of the things you identified, as you begin to outline and compose your essay. It keeps you involved in the passage as well. Remember, taking the SAT is like a marathon. You need to pace yourself and plan your attack. By the time you get to the essay, you may be on your last leg. If you sit down to read that last passage, you may find yourself getting lost and maybe floating in and out of the actual reading. If you give yourself tasks such as underlining, it will keep you in the game. The reason that active reading strategies are effective is that you are essentially creating yourself a key. This key will save you tons of time as you begin to write. Instead of having to skim and scan your way back through the essay with every point you write, you can easily find your evidence and stick to your plan. This is something you will need to practice so you know what works best for you.

Gathering Evidence

The SAT considers the following as sources of evidence: facts, statistics, examples or quotes. Let's look back at the passage we used earlier. We already recognized that the purpose of this passage is to inform. An informative passage is built on evidence. If you have labeled the passage as you read, this evidence should be easy to find. Skimming the passage, statistics, quotes and anecdotes are not pieces of evidence that are used. What the author does use is examples. The cadence of the paragraphs is fairly uniform: the author provides a tip and then an example of how that can be implemented. Here are three examples supporting the provided tips:

Tip: Dedicate yourself to savings

Example: The key to making that financial transformation is a dedicated savings plan, to ensure that you continue to pursue your end results.

Tip: small savings matter

Example: If you are looking for a one percent increase, saying no to a hundred-dollar dinner might achieve just that.

Tip: Seek help

Example: A financial advisor knows the rules and ropes of the retirement industry and can point you towards real savings.

Now let's put it together:

The purpose of this passage is to show you that saving for retirement is possible. The author builds the argument through a selection of tips which are supported by examples. These examples provide real world applications of the tips that the author is suggesting.

That is the core of the argument and a good start for your essay. Remember, you also need to discuss the main idea and details and how they are working together to flesh out this argument. This can be done by referencing the topic and showing how the details are used to explain it. Here is an example:

The author uses realistic examples to explain to the reader how saving for retirement is possible.

This tells the scorer that you know the main idea as you are also introducing an argumentative technique used in your analysis.

Reasoning

Let's now talk about reasoning and the rhetorical devices that are used to put together a compelling piece of writing. The use of rhetorical devices is specifically related to how the reasoning is developed and typically the concepts of logos, pathos and ethos are used to discuss this element of argument.

In case you are unsure here is a quick overview of the three concepts:

❑ **Logos:** Logos is referenced as method of development when you use facts or statistics to convince the audience. An argument utilizing logos is typically logical argument and appeals to the reader who needs to see statistics, facts and graphs to be convinced. So, when you reference logos think of the analytical reader who typically wants information and news as their primary reading diet.

❑ **Pathos:** This argument is based upon an emotional appeal to the reader. These arguments create moments of feeling that compel the reader to take action, be afraid, feel empathy or find joy in the writing. Regardless of the particular emotion, the reader is moved by feelings rather than logic. Many of the most memorable political speeches are written on a pathos platform.

❑ **Ethos:** This is an argument built on the believability of the author. The reader typically chooses the piece based on the credibility of the author rather than topic. The purpose of these pieces can be informative, persuasive or entertaining, but the focal point is the author. Essentially, the reader buys into the argument because of their belief in the veracity of the author.

Let's return to the passage. In case of this passage, logos would be best fit if you were to describe the reasoning device used. The author is unknown, so that rules out ethos and because this is an informative piece, there is no appeal to emotions so, you can also rule out pathos.

Now let's find evidence to support the logos approach.

a) We can first reference the examples approach that we have already identified.

b) We can also use these examples that are built in the form of advice:

Example one: *So, with the help of an expert, a close look at your budget and a long view of a savings plan, you can really succeed in creating a sustainable retirement plan.*

Example two: *Of course, there are items such as bills and mortgage payments that can't be forgone, but even cancelling one night out is a wise place to start.*

Example three: *Instead, look at the year-to-year comparison to see the difference your dedicated savings is making to your retirement's bottom line.*

This advice helps the reader build a plan of attack as they demonstrate the feasibility of starting a small savings plan to yield big results.

Style

Style refers to how the passage is put together, how it sounds, how it impacts the reader and how it uses literary devices to tell its story. Speaking of literary devices, that is a good place to start if you are considering using style as a point of analysis. Refer to the literary devices section to learn more about those most common to the SAT Essay. The second thing to listen for is how this piece would sound if it were read aloud. In other words, what is the author's tone? Is this an academic piece? Is it funny? Each tone impacts audience as it influences the way the author interacts with the reader and how the author shapes the argument that is presented therein.

To get to the heart of style, investigate how the author speaks to the audience. In this passage, the author uses a first-person approach with the pronouns of "we", "us" and "you." By doing this, the author is speaking directly to the reader. This makes the reader feel as though the piece is written directly for them. This helps the reader feel the feasibility of this plan and increases their buy-in. To evidence this point, you can point to any time the author uses my, us and you. In this instance, mentioning it to the scorer or naming a line is enough. Again, don't waste your time copying full sentences that contain these pronouns.

The next stylistic device that the author uses is to employ questions to directly involve the reader.

One example of this is when the author asks: *"Do I really need this?"*

Finally take a look at the overall tone of the piece. Remember, this is how the piece would sound if it were read aloud. Is this piece formal, academic, full of technical investing language? No. In this case the passage is very informal. So, you can say that the language is informal to engage the average reader while convincing them that this route is feasible for anyone.

Now, back up your contention with evidence. Find examples of relaxed language. Any of these examples would be sufficient. Look for language that is colloquial, relaxed or sounds like dialogue.

a) drop of rain in the ocean

b) wise

c) key

d) you'll make it

e) even the tightest budget

Now that you have all this identified, your craft is how you put it all together to tell the story of the passage. Choose components that not only prove your points but also work with the reading task to present an overall view of why this piece works with its readers and why its argument has impact and flow.

Keep it Simple

The first tip is to write with coherence. What this simply means is that people should be able to understand what you write. Creating complicated overly complex sentences does nothing for your score.

Look at these two examples and ask yourself which one you would rather read.

Example one: *The author emphasizes humor to help tell the story of the elephant.*

Example two: *In the telling of the overly emphasized story of the lone element, the humorous language is used well.*

The first one gets to the point and clearly points out what and why is happening.

The first one is also an example of active language. Write in a way that tells what is going on now. Don't tell the scorer what did happen or what will happen. Active language is key to a good score.

Agreement

The second strategy is to make sure your subject and verbs agree. This seems like a minor point, but it is also a red flag for scorers and jumps out as a common error.

Look at these two examples

Example one: *The author write strongly about the main focus of the game.*

Example two: *The author writes strongly about the main focus of the game.*

Which one sounds right to you? The second one is correct. 'One' author goes with writes not write. If you are confused on this topic, there are lots of great grammar tutorials online that can help you learn the basics.

Another red flag is misuse of adverbs. Adverbs are words that describe verbs and unlike adjective which proceed and describe nouns, adverbs typically follow verbs and usually end with an ly.

Here is a very common example of an adverb misused:

Example: *Drive careful.*

The correct usage of the adverb "careful" is *Drive carefully.*

Correct use of adverbs can score you big points as it demonstrates advanced writing techniques.

Sentence Structure

Another thing to consider, especially as you edit, is how you vary your sentence structure. Are your sentences all simple and short? Are they all complex and long? Neither is advisable. The best writing is that which is varied, so your reader's mind can follow a varied path.

Try these two short passages..

The author uses logos. Evidence is used to support this. The evidence is quotes and statistics. The argument is clear.

The author, using a variety of approaches which include logos, also uses supporting quote and statistics in a meaningful way. To further clarify the argument, which is both emotionally and logically inspiring, the author must provide the reader their own path of enjoyment.

Both pieces are hard to read. The first is like driving a car with bump after bump after bump. The second is like driving a car when you never get a break. You are searching for that stop sign and it is just never there.

Here is a good example.

Example: The author uses logos to develop his arguments. He uses the statement in sentence one to support the focus of the argument through the use of statistics.

Vocabulary

One of the most substantial things you can do to improve your score is to concentrate on a purposeful use of advanced vocabulary. First, it is essential that you use transition words. Here are some great words that not only increase the interest in your essay but also help organize it.

❑ **Cause and effect vocabulary:** consequently, therefore, accordingly, as a result, because, for this reason, hence, thus

❑ **Sequencing:** furthermore, in addition, moreover, first, second, third, finally, again, also, and, besides, further, in the first place, last

❑ **Compare or contrast vocabulary:** similarly, also, in the same way, likewise, although, at the same time, but, conversely, even so, however, in contrast, nevertheless, nonetheless, notwithstanding

Next, there are some common words that are used in this type of writing. They are great words to learn and use in all of your writing. In fact, the internet is littered with the SAT word lists which offer a great place to start building your vocabulary. But use these words with caution. If you think you can just sprinkle in a few "big" words and score big points, you are mistaken. Let's take the word plethora for example. This is a great word, and it means a lot. But it is a very formal word and doesn't apply to every situation when you have a lot of this or that. It sounds out of place in essays with otherwise more informal language. Make sure that whatever words you are using; you are using them correctly.

Here are some words to learn and use to up the word choice score.

Abstract	Not concrete or real
Aesthetic	A view point that is artistic
Alleviate	To make better
Ambivalent	No strong feelings
Benevolent	Good
Cogent	Well-reasoned
Conviction	Strong beliefs
Diligent	Hard working
Gratuitous	Too much
Impartial	Not one side or another
Innovative	Bringing something new
Novel	New
Objectivity	No emotion in decisions
Ornate	Overly decorative
Paramount	Very important
Pervasive	Throughout
Plausible	Could happened
Profound	Depth
Quandary	a question
Spurious	Not genuine
Superfluous	Not necessary
Vindicated	Freed from blame

Literary devices to use for writing a good essay

Here are some common devices and how they might be used.

- ❑ **Anecdote:** These take the form of a short story. They can be used in entertaining pieces to help forward the story and create an emotional impact or in a persuasive passage to help move the reader to change your perspective.

- ❑ **Allusion:** An allusion is a reference to another piece: movie, song, poem, or piece of writing. This can be used as evidence, to increase the emotional appeal or to prove a point.

- ❑ **Testimony:** Testimonies are usually used to prove a point or gain credibility. These are particularly used in informative or persuasive pieces.

- ❑ **Statistics and Data:** These facts and figures should be a component of a piece of writing with strong logos.

- ❑ **Rhetorical Questions:** Rhetorical questions are meant to make the reader think. They act as a point to involve the reader but are not intended to actually elicit an answer. In other words, the answer is implied. They are often used as hooks for informative or persuasive pieces of writing.

- ❑ **Metaphor:** A metaphor creates a comparison that literally says one thing is another thing. Metaphors are used as stylistic devices to increase readers' interest.

- ❑ **Simile:** A simile is a comparison that says one thing is like another. This is another stylistic device.

- ❑ **Personification:** Personification is when a non-human thing is given human characteristics. Think Disney! It is usually done to inspire empathy and elicit some kind of emotional response.

- ❑ **Hyperbole:** Hyperbole is an exaggerated statement. Watch for this device in persuasive pieces. Often, authors will inflate claims to make their argument seem more believable or move the reader to action with more urgency.

- ❑ **Symbolism:** Symbolism is when one thing represents something else. This is a stylistic device that may not be prevalent in the essays you will read on the SAT. This is more common in fictional pieces.

- ❑ **Imagery:** This language helps the reader use their senses to experience a moment or point of view. It is used as a stylistic element and helps involve the reader in the vision of the piece of writing.

- ❑ **Diction:** Diction is basically word choice. For the purpose of the SAT ask yourself if the diction or tone of the piece is academic, formal, informal, and check if it includes technical language or slang. This will help you define purpose and intended audience.

- ❑ **Jargon:** Jargon is language associated with a particular field or occupation. It can be seen as technical or casual and as a stylistic device can help illuminate the purpose and intended audience.

- ❑ **Repetition:** Mentioning a word or phrase several times prompts prominence. If an idea or a word is repeated, the reader will remember it. Repetition is often seen in persuasive pieces to help focus an issue.

❑ **Juxtaposition:** Juxtaposition means to compare or contrast. This is a strong tool in an argument because the author shows their consideration of both sides of the issue.

❑ **Antithesis:** Mentioning one thing and its opposite. This again adds to the author's sense of comparison and can add to the strength and veracity of the argument.

❑ **Inclusive Language:** Inclusive language helps the reader feel like they are part of the group. Using first or second person language allows the reader to feel as though they are important and included in the solution. Look for personal pronouns to help target this inclusive language.

❑ **Tone:** Tone is the way the author's voice sounds. This can be used as a stylistic device and can also help define the overall purpose of the piece.

Practice and Plan

The last strategy is to practice. You need to know how much time you will need to read and which strategies work best for you. There are many examples of passages available from the College Board. Also, ample practice in terms of sample passages and prompts, is provided in Chapter 3. Get used to these passages' formats, voices and tones and the way they use language. Although each passage is different, they are all written at the same reading level and most are a similar length. Getting used to the genre, tone and length is a huge task in your practice. Remember, you are not reading to gain information or enjoy the reading passage. You are reading to get the evidence you need to construct your essay. This type of reading requires practice and a strategic approach. The more you practice, the easier it will seem as you sit down to embark on the essay "for real."

This page is intentionally left blank

Chapter 3
Solved Essays

This chapter covers **16 Solved Essay prompts.** Each essay is broken into three parts:

❑ Prompt: includes the prompt and the passage

❑ Pre-Essay Writing: includes the strategies to be used to develop a top-scoring essay

❑ Sample Essay: includes a sample essay written for reference

Based on the strategies explained in the Pre-Essay writing and the sample essay, write your own essay in the space provided after the Sample Essay. The essay gives you an opportunity to show how effectively you can read and comprehend a passage and write an essay analyzing the passage. In your essay, you should demonstrate that you have read the passage carefully, present a clear and logical analysis, and use language precisely. Remember that people who are not familiar with your handwriting will read what you write. Try to write or print so that what you are writing is legible to those readers.

You have 50 minutes to read the passage and write an essay in response to the prompt provided.

Essay 1

Prompt

As you read the passage below, consider how Chandler uses

❑ evidence, such as facts or examples, to support claims.

❑ reasoning to develop ideas and to connect claims and evidence.

❑ stylistic or persuasive elements, such as word choice or appeals to emotion, to add power to the ideas expressed.

Adapted from Adam Chandler, "Nothing Can Replace the Bodega" ©2017 by The New York Times. Originally published September 13, 2017.

1. Like solar eclipses and bipartisan legislation, moments of near-universal consensus are extremely rare. One such event took place on Wednesday, when a start-up named Bodega stated its intention to put its name-sake - real-life, neighborhood corner stores - out of business by replacing them with unmanned pantries.

2. "Eventually, centralized shopping locations won't be necessary, because there will be 100,000 Bodegas spread out, with one always 100 feet away from you," one of its co-founders told Fast Company. The start-up, run by two ex-Googlers, was widely savaged across social media on the grounds that its name and business mission are culturally insensitive, morally dubious, and, perhaps worse of all, lack personality.

3. Few things make a New Yorker defensive like an assault on bodegas. Largely immigrant-owned, they are the ultimate frills-free symbol of consumer access and gritty mini-embodiments of both the city's diversity and its 24/7 ethos. Bacon, egg, and cheese sandwiches in the morning, basic groceries and oversized heroes in the afternoon, and, inevitably, all three of these things at 3 a.m.

4. In other words, a bodega has crucial provisions whenever you need them, judgment-free and generally at a small-to-medium markup. Alka-Seltzer, regular seltzer, Gatorade, and Advil. Toilet paper and deodorant. Tampons and condoms. Last winter, a bodega on the Lower East Side gained a small measure of fame or notoriety when it was reported that customers could order Plan B pills online and have them delivered to their apartments.

5. But in addition to their convenience, what make bodegas beloved are their personalities. It seems like every one of them is oddly curated: prayer candles sit next to jarred olives which are sidled up next to boxes organic mac-and-cheese. There is no Silicon Valley algorithm clever enough to come up with those crumbly, shrink-wrapped date bars that are inevitably piled up by the cash registers.

6. Michael Silber is a graphic designer who has documented over 1,200 New York City bodegas over the past three years for Deli Grossery, a project whose name is a nod to the iconic and idiosyncratic food signage outside of corner stores. "For me, bodegas and deli groceries really encapsulate the character and culture of a neighborhood," Mr. Silber noted in an email. "Each has its own delicacies or quirks, whether it be a famous chopped cheese sandwich, unfamiliar Polish specialty foods, or a friendly bodega cat." (Further fanning the flames for Bodega is that the company logo is a cat, an unlawful fixture and unofficial mascot of many corner stores.)

7. Of course, the most meaningful difference between Wi-Fi-enabled vending machines and family-run corner stores is the human being. Corner stores aren't just a small compensation for living in a dense city. They also enable countless New Yorkers to begin their day with routines that are both rote and reassuring, whether it's a buttered roll, a cup of coffee, or a sane, friendly encounter.

8. A well-cultivated, strategic relationship with your bodega can mean that you might have a safe place for your spare keys and packages. If you're really lucky, the clerks will share their life stories with you, tell you about all the ways you're screwing up your romantic life, and remember that you add American cheese to everything.

9. My first bodega in New York was on 8th Avenue, where I was known as "Houston" by the staff because, well, I'm from Houston. Of course, it was pronounced like the nearby street in Lower Manhattan rather than the city in Texas. At first, it irritated me to no end. Then I realized, it was a way of letting me know that I had arrived.

10. Many years later, my current bodega opened on my block in Brooklyn a year after I had moved in. Their shelves were still half-stocked at their grand opening. When I asked if there would be date bars, they told me to come back tomorrow. It doesn't get more high-tech than that.

• •

Write an essay in which you explain how Chandler builds an argument to persuade his audience that bodegas can never be replaced. In your essay, analyze how Chandler uses one or more of the features listed above (or features of your own choice) to strengthen the logic and persuasiveness of his argument. Be sure that your analysis focuses on the most relevant features of the passage.

Your essay should not explain whether you agree with Chandler's claims, but rather explain how the author builds an argument to persuade his audience.

• •

Pre-Essay Writing

Read the essay prompt before you read the provided text. Make sure you have a firm grasp on what the prompt is asking you to analyze in your essay. In this case, the prompt specifically says, "explain how Chandler builds an argument to persuade his audience that bodegas can never be replaced". A keyword here is "how".

How does Chandler persuade his audience? Recall the bullet points already given to you, asking you to notice evidence such as facts, statistics, or reliable experience, reasoning that connects ideas through logic and explanation, and stylistic or persuasive elements such as word choice, emotional appeal, building credibility, etc. Chandler's techniques will show up in his body paragraphs. As you read, take note of Chandler's use of these things and begin to mentally map out your essay.

Some examples from Chandler's text:

Facts

a) "A start-up named Bodega stated its intention to put its namesake - real-life, neighborhood corner stores - out of business by replacing them with unmanned pantries."

b) "The start-up, run by two ex-Googlers, was widely savaged across social media on the grounds that its name and business mission are culturally insensitive, morally dubious, and, perhaps worse of all, lack personality."

c) "Michael Silber is a graphic designer who has documented over 1,200 New York City bodegas over the past three years for Deli Grossery, a project whose name is a nod to the iconic and idiosyncratic food signage outside of corner stores."

d) "Last winter, a bodega on the Lower East Side gained a small measure of fame or notoriety when it was reported that customers could order Plan B pills online and have them delivered to their apartments."

Reasoning

a) "In other words, a bodega has crucial provisions whenever you need them, judgment-free and generally at a small-to-medium markup."

b) "There is no Silicon Valley algorithm clever enough to come up with those crumbly, shrink-wrapped date bars that are inevitably piled up by the cash registers."

c) "Of course, the most meaningful difference between Wi-Fi-enabled vending machines and family-run corner stores is the human being."

d) "A well-cultivated, strategic relationship with your bodega can mean that you might have a safe place for your spare keys and packages.

Stylistic Elements

a) **Descriptive words:** "savaged," "frills-free," "gritty," "beloved," "oddly," etc.

b) **Fragments:** "Bacon, egg, and cheese sandwiches in the morning, basic groceries and oversized heroes in the afternoon, and, inevitably, all three of these things at 3 a.m." "Alka-Seltzer, regular seltzer, Gatorade, and Advil. Toilet paper and deodorant. Tampons and condoms." Etc.

c) **Clear transitions:** "Of course," "In other words," "But in addition to their convenience," "Last winter," etc.

Persuasive Elements

a) **Emotional appeal:** "Of course, the most meaningful difference between Wi-Fi-enabled vending machines and family-run corner stores is the human being. Corner stores aren't just a small compensation for living in a dense city. They also enable countless New Yorkers to begin their day with routines that are both rote and reassuring, whether it's a buttered roll, a cup of coffee, or a sane, friendly encounter." etc.

b) **Humor:** "If you're really lucky, the clerks will share their life stories with you, tell you about all the ways you're screwing up your romantic life, and remember that you add American cheese to everything." etc.

c) **Credibility:** "savaged across social media," ""For me, bodegas and deli groceries really encapsulate the character and culture of a neighborhood," Mr. Silber noted in an email," etc.

Thoroughly read through the entire text given, paying special attention to key points. You will only have time for one full read through. Key points will be quickly exposed through a thesis-like statement and topic sentences. An author's thesis statement most often appears in the introductory paragraph and sometimes title. In Chandler's case, the title is the only blatant mention of his thesis. Throughout body of the article, his thesis is strongly implied.

Chandler's Thesis:

"Nothing Can Replace the Bodega" and *"Few things make a New Yorker defensive like an assault on bodegas. Largely immigrant-owned, they are the ultimate frills-free symbol of consumer access and gritty mini-embodiments of both the city's diversity and its 24/7 ethos."*

Chandler's Topic Sentences:

Topic sentences are the first sentence of every paragraph.

"'Eventually, centralized shopping locations won't be necessary, because there will be 100,000 Bodegas spread out, with one always 100 feet away from you,' one of its co-founders told Fast Company."

"Few things make a New Yorker defensive like an assault on bodegas."

"In other words, a bodega has crucial provisions whenever you need them, judgment-free and generally at a small-to-medium markup."

"But in addition to their convenience, what make bodegas beloved are their personalities."

Etc.

The author's key points will be the structure that your own key points mimic. In this case, Chandler's key points are rising convenience and personality, human interaction, and widespread familiarity. Analyze these points for persuasive techniques, and you have a list of reasons, emotional appeal, and agreeing voices/credibility. These three things are the "how" that the sample essay chooses to focus on, but Chandler uses other techniques (like those examples given above), as well, to persuade his audience. No two essays will be alike as you and your peers will analyze Chandler's work through a personal lens.

Create a clear and concise thesis that states the author's persuasive techniques.

Sample essay's thesis: *He supports his claim by citing evidence of necessity, making relatable emotional appeals, and calling up agreeing voices.*

For detailed analysis, these techniques could reasonably be a list of 2-4 (3, in the sample essay's case). One essay style is to focus each body paragraph on one of those techniques. Another style would be to summarize like techniques in paragraphs together. Paraphrase and quote a few specific lines from the text that support your analysis. Keep any quotes used relatively short. Make sure to always surround a quote with your own words. Introduce the quote, include the quote, and then clearly explain why this quote shows the author's persuasive technique. The essay should be mostly your words, not the authors.

Conclude your essay by pointing out the author's intentions, along with their specific audience. Avoid merely restating your thesis.

Sample essay: *There's no room for a machined pantry because, as Chandler argues, the corner store is needed for its convenience, its diversity, its personality; it speaks to the heart, and almost everyone agrees with him. Chandler wants the founders of "Bodega" to know where they truly stand, but it's the people, his readers, that really have a say on what stays.*

Answer Sheet

Use a No. 2 pencil. Begin your essay on this page. If you need more space, continue on the next page.

_____

_____

_____

_____

_____

_____

_____

_____

_____

1

1

Sample Essay

Adam Chandler, in his article "Nothing Can Replace the Bodega," expresses a clear passion for the old, familiar charm of the neighborhood corner store. After hearing of the possible extinction of those bodegas due to a mechanized "Bodega" start-up, Chandler argues that a robot pantry can never replace a true neighborhood bodega. He supports his claim by citing evidence of necessity, making relatable emotional appeals, and calling up agreeing voices.

Chandler has an arsenal of reasons for why the original neighborhood bodegas are not only unbeatable but also a necessity. He launches into a long list of reasons, starting with its symbolism of "consumer access" and "mini-embodiment of cultural diversity," meaning that the corner store is a nice source of income for some, especially immigrants. He goes on to list that each bodega has a variety of items conveniently available at all times of the day (paragraph 4), a set of unique personalities (paragraph 5), a chance for human interaction (paragraph 7), and a comforting familiarity (paragraph 8). With each item in the list, Chandler aims to remind the reader that these are all things we need in life. He talks about them with an air of nostalgia, harkening back and holding onto the pleasantries of the past, not the "Silicon Valley algorithms" of the future. He also makes a point of necessity by packing all of this evidence in so few words.

For a diversified approach, Chandler takes time in his logical list to use emotional appeal on his audience. Chandler refers to the start-up "Bodega" as "unmanned pantries," "algorithms," and "Wi-Fi-enabled vending machines". He does this to paint a cold and impersonal picture of the start-up versus the warm and personal picture of corner stores, whose words are more like "beloved," "character," and "reassuring". He continues to try and get readers to feel something for bodegas by reminding them of its unfaltering reliance; a specific list of items these stores carry includes, "Alka-Seltzer, regular seltzer, Gatorade, and Advil. Toilet paper and deodorant. Tampons and condoms". Chandler pointedly picks these items because they are, more than likely, items that the reader has purchased from a corner store during a time of dire need. Additionally, the people of neighborhood bodegas are familiar and friendly. Chandler mentions scenarios reminiscent of "a place where everybody knows your name" to sound homey.

Lastly, Chandler wants the readers and "Bodega" founders to know that he's not the only one who favors the original bodega. He explains that after the initial announcement of the start-up, the idea was "savaged across social media". Chandler uses a strong word such as "savage" to make it clear that there are many people who were more than a little upset at the potential loss of the corner store. He even makes what is supposed to be a truthful quip about a rare "near-universal consensus" about bodegas winning out of the "Bodega". He also calls on Michael Silber who has documented more than 1,200 New York bodegas and who echoes Chandler's sentiments of neighborhood culture and charming quirkiness. Essentially, Chandler shows that he has an expert on his side. With each mention of an agreeing voice, Chandler increases his credibility to the reader.

In a technology-forward society, an unmanned "Bodega" seems fitting, but Chandler fights against this idea. There's no room for a machined pantry because, as Chandler argues, the corner store is needed for its convenience, its diversity, its personality; it speaks to the heart, and almost everyone agrees with him. Chandler wants the founders of "Bodega" to know where they truly stand, but it's the people, his readers, that really have a say on what stays.

Essay 2

Prompt

As you read the passage below, consider how the Editorial Board uses

- ❑ evidence, such as facts or examples, to support claims.

- ❑ reasoning to develop ideas and to connect claims and evidence.

- ❑ stylistic or persuasive elements, such as word choice or appeals to emotion, to add power to the ideas expressed.

Adapted from Editorial Board, "How many women run major companies? Not enough"
©2017 by Chicago Tribune. Originally published September 18, 2017.

1. Ilene Gordon announced her retirement Monday as one of the most important Chicago-area CEOs you've never heard of: Her west suburban company, Ingredion, makes ingredients for other food companies, so if you like your pop to taste sweet or your baked tortilla chips to be crunchy, you can thank her.

2. That's one reason to take note of Gordon's departure. The other reason is that she is a valuable role model, one of the few female leaders at the nation's 500 largest companies.

3. Gordon will be succeeded by Jim Zallie, thus reducing the ranks of female CEOs at Fortune 500 companies. This repeats the circumstances at another big food company, Deerfield-based Mondelez International, the maker of Oreo cookies and Ritz crackers. At Mondelez, CEO Irene Rosenfeld also will be succeeded by a man, Dirk Van de Put.

4. How many female CEOs would you guess are at the helm of Fortune 500 companies? At last count there were 32, including Gordon and Rosenfeld. That means just 6 percent of the nation's highest-profile CEOs are women. That's shockingly low representation, more so because Fortune said in June that 32 women in the top spots was a record high for the list. There were 21 female CEOs at Fortune 500 companies in 2016.

5. Women make up almost half the overall workforce. They do well in the white-collar world, as long as it's fields such as human resources (74 percent of positions) and marketing and sales management (46 percent). The numbers begin to drop off after that, according to the U.S. Department of Labor: 27 percent of CEOs are women and 26 percent of computer and information systems managers are women.

6. One could look at the trends, including the jump from 21 female Fortune 500 CEOs, and surmise that the current generation of women in business is poised to reach the top spots in much greater numbers. If 27 percent of all CEOs are women, why not 27 percent of Fortune 500 CEOS? Why not 50 percent - and soon? Then again, women have been poised to break through for years, and still they face workplace obstacles

rooted in sexism and discrimination.

7. One recent example was the scandal at Uber, where CEO Travis Kalanick lost his job for overseeing a toxic work environment in which a female engineer was propositioned on her first day of a new assignment, and got the cold shoulder from H.R.

8. Uber reportedly sought a female leader to replace Kalanick, and interviewed Meg Whitman of Hewlett Packard Enterprise, but ultimately it hired a man, Dara Khosrowshahi of Expedia. The hiring search generated the classic headline "Uber's search for a female CEO has been narrowed down to 3 men." Snarky, and possibly accurate, but it's also possible Khosrowshahi was the right person for the job at Uber.

9. The expectation that more women should be running the biggest companies is rooted in the basic idea of equality: Men and women both bring talents to the workforce and should have equal chances to lead their organizations. The need is to create a level playing field for all candidates, not obsess over each company's hiring decisions. Which brings us back to Ilene Gordon, who transformed Ingredion by diversifying the company beyond its roots as a maker of high-fructose corn syrup to focus on ingredients that help improve the texture of foods. She built Ingredion's fortunes. She was the right person for the job, the way Zallie may be the right person to succeed her.

10. Gordon said in a 2013 Wall Street Journal interview that she hired for her management team based on ability. But she also insisted on seeing a diverse slate of candidates for each position. That diversity "might be cultural, it could be gender. But if you don't have them on the slate of possible candidates, you're never going to get there."

11. She expanded on that view Monday in a Tribune interview: "I'm a big believer in building the pipeline and we will get there. You will see more women as leaders of Fortune 500 companies," she predicted.

12. Gordon is a role model, as is Rosenfeld. We hope to see many women follow their paths.

Write an essay in which you explain how the Editorial Board builds an argument to persuade their audience that women need the same opportunity as men to make it as a Fortune 500 CEO. In your essay, analyze how the Board uses one or more of the features listed above (or features of your own choice) to strengthen the logic and persuasiveness of his argument. Be sure that your analysis focuses on the most relevant features of the passage.

Your essay should not explain whether you agree with the Board's claims, but rather explain how the author builds an argument to persuade its audience.

Pre-Essay Writing

Read the essay prompt before you read the provided text. Make sure you have a firm grasp on what the prompt is asking you to analyze in your essay. In this case, the prompt specifically says, "explain how the Editorial Board builds an argument to persuade their audience that women need the same opportunity as men to make it as a Fortune 500 CEO". A keyword here is "how". How does the Board persuade its audience? Recall the bullet points already given to you, asking you to notice evidence such as facts, statistics, or reliable experience, reasoning that connects ideas through logic and explanation, and stylistic or persuasive elements such as word choice, emotional appeal, building credibility, etc. The Board's techniques will show up in the body paragraphs. As you read, take note of the Board's use of these things and begin to mentally map out your essay.

Some examples from the Board's text:

Facts

a) "Ilene Gordon announced her retirement Monday as one of the most important Chicago-area CEOs you've never heard of."

b) "At Mondelez, CEO Irene Rosenfeld also will be succeeded by a man, Dirk Van de Put."

c) "There were 21 female CEOs at Fortune 500 companies in 2016."

d) "Uber reportedly sought a female leader to replace Kalanick, and interviewed Meg Whitman of Hewlett Packard Enterprise, but ultimately it hired a man, Dara Khosrowshahi of Expedia."

Statistics

a) "At last count there were 32, including Gordon and Rosenfeld."

b) "That means just 6 percent of the nation's highest-profile CEOs are women."

c) "They do well in the white-collar world, as long as it's fields such as human resources (74 percent of positions) and marketing and sales management (46 percent)."

d) "The numbers begin to drop off after that, according to the U.S. Department of Labor: 27 percent of CEOs are women and 26 percent of computer and information systems managers are women."

Reasoning

a) "Gordon will be succeeded by Jim Zallie, thus reducing the ranks of female CEOs at Fortune 500 companies."

b) "That's shockingly low representation, more so because Fortune said in June that 32 women in the top spots was a record high for the list."

c) "If 27 percent of all CEOs are women, why not 27 percent of Fortune 500 CEOS? Why not 50 percent -and soon?"

d) "She was the right person for the job, the way Zallie may be the right person to succeed her."

Stylistic Elements

a) Qualifiers: "just," "as long as," "then again," "still," etc.

b) Contradicting word choice: "classic" versus "basic".

c) Positive word choice: "equal," "level playing field," "based on ability," "diversity," etc.

Persuasive Elements

a) Examples: Ilene Gordon, Irene Rosenfeld, Uber's H.R., stats, etc.

b) Quotes: "might be cultural, it could be gender. But if you don't have them on the slate of possible candidates, you're never going to get there," "I'm a big believer in building the pipeline and we will get there. You will see more women as leaders of Fortune 500 companies," "Uber's search for a female CEO has been narrowed down to 3 men," etc.

c) Credibility: "Men and women both bring talents to the workforce and should have equal chances to lead their organizations." "She was the right person for the job, the way Zallie may be the right person to succeed her." Etc.

Thoroughly read through the entire text given, paying special attention to key points. You will only have time for one full read through. Key points will be quickly exposed through a thesis-like statement and topic sentences. An author's thesis statement most often appears in the introductory paragraph and/or title. The Board's thesis is in the title and implied throughout the essay.

The Board's Thesis:

(Title) *How many women run major companies? Not enough*

(Implied) *If 27 percent of all CEOs are women, why not 27 percent of Fortune 500 CEOS? Why not 50 percent — and soon?*

The Board's Topic sentences:

Topic sentences are the first sentence of every paragraph.

"That's one reason to take note of Gordon's departure."

"How many female CEOs would you guess are at the helm of Fortune 500 companies?"

"Women make up almost half the overall workforce."

"One could look at the trends, including the jump from 21 female Fortune 500 CEOs, and surmise that the current generation of women in business is poised to reach the top spots in much greater numbers."

Etc.

The author's key points will be the structure that your own key points mimic. In this case, the Board's key points are a large gap between men and women CEOs, the negativity of this gap, the equal abilities of men and women. Analyze these points for persuasive techniques, and you have statistics, stylistic word choices, and persuasive facts that build credibility. These three things are the "how" that the sample essay chooses to focus on, but Upton uses other techniques (like those examples given above), as well, to persuade his audience. No two essays will be alike as you and your peers will analyze the Board's work through a personal lens.

Create a clear and concise thesis that states the author's persuasive techniques.

Sample essay's thesis: *They support their claim by showing disparity in statistics, making clear connections with stylistic choices, and providing undeniably persuasive facts.*

For detailed analysis, these techniques could reasonably be a list of 2-4 (3, in the sample essay's case). One essay style is to focus each body paragraph on one of those techniques. Another style would be to summarize like techniques in paragraphs together. Paraphrase and quote a few specific lines from the text that support your analysis. Keep any quotes used relatively short. Make sure to always surround a quote with your own words. Introduce the quote, include the quote, and then clearly explain why this quote shows the author's persuasive technique. The essay should be mostly your words, not the authors.

Conclude your essay by pointing out the author's intentions, along with their specific audience. Avoid merely restating your thesis.

2

Sample essay: *It's an honor and an impressive accomplishment to be at the top of a Fortune 500, but half the US popu-lation isn't getting a good shot at that honor. The Editorial Board at the Chicago Tribune supports the controversial belief that there aren't enough women by providing undeniable statistics and facts and linking them to their claim with stylistic word choice. Their readers, men and women, especially those in hiring positions, should create equal opportunity hiring to support basic rights and strong companies.*

Answer Sheet

Use a No. 2 pencil. Begin your essay on this page. If you need more space, continue on the next page.

_____

_____

_____

_____

_____

_____

_____

_____

_____

_____

_____

_____

_____

_____

_____

_____

_____

_____

_____

_____

2

2

Sample Essay

It's every business's grand dream to make it as a Fortune 500 company, and every entrepreneur's grand dream to climb up the ladder of a Fortune 500 company. At the moment, though, the list of those top ladder-climbers is largely dominated by men. According to the Editorial Board of The Chicago Tribune, women need the same opportunity as men to make it as a Fortune 500 CEO. They support their claim by showing disparity in statistics, making clear connections with stylistic choices, and providing undeniably persuasive facts.

The Board front-loads their argument by showing supportive statistic, after supportive statistic. Citing that there are only 32 female CEO's out of the Fortune 500 companies, a whopping 6%, the Board hopes this large difference is a shock to the reader. They go on to supply more context. "[Women] do well in the white-collar world, as long as it's fields such as human resources (74 percent of positions) and marketing and sales management (46 percent)." The contrast between the high percentages of the human resources and marketing worlds versus the low percentage of high-profile CEOs is again, another large disparity. In fact, the Board makes an even closer comparison with the US Department of Labor's statement that women CEOs (of any business) make up 21%. The Board uses all of these statistics to show its readers that, while women often have lower percentages than men, high-profile CEOs are by far the worst. Even the numbers show there aren't enough women.

Beyond sheer statistics, the Board crafts their article with a writing style that connects careful word choice to conclusions that work in their favor. One way the Board does this is with qualifiers. Sure, women are successful "as long as" they are in certain fields; 32 women is "just" 6%; statistics have improved, but "still" they face obstacles. The Board uses these qualifiers to subtly show the reader that success for women at a high level is the exception, not the rule. The Board also uses careful word choice when showing the difference of an outdated cultural mindset to a more modern mindset. They point out that a "classic" headline reads, "Uber's search for a female CEO has been narrowed down to 3 men." This outcome is "classic," "expected". However, running successful companies is a "basic" idea of equality. The Board shows the reader the contradiction of what is "classic" and "basic". They solidify their style by attaching positive words to women in the workplace, throughout the article. Words like, "level playing field," "based on ability," and "diversity" associate a positive feeling in the reader to the movement of equality.

Lastly, the Board has many examples and points of credibility that work to persuade the reader that women are undervalued. Two examples are Ilene Gordon and Irene Rosenfeld, both female CEOs of Fortune 500 companies that got replaced by men. Another example arose when Uber aimed to hire a woman after firing their CEO for sexual harassment. They ultimately hired a man. The Board includes these examples to show that, though, women excel, companies aren't necessarily recognizing it. The confidence these examples seeks to instill in readers is enhanced when the Board gives mutual respect to men. They aren't men-haters; in fact, they state that both sexes bring talent to the workforce and should have equal hiring opportunity. This unbiased approach gives them credibility with their audience. Quotes they include in the article increase this trustworthiness, as well. They quote Gordon as saying that diversity could be a lot of things, including gender, but you'll never hire diversely if you don't give them the chance. The Board even uses one of those past female CEOs to show that the high-level hiring situation can be unbiased and equal.

It's an honor and an impressive accomplishment to be at the top of a Fortune 500, but half the US population isn't getting a good shot at that honor. The Editorial Board at the Chicago Tribune supports the controversial belief that there aren't enough women by providing undeniable statistics and facts and linking them to their claim with stylistic word choice. Their readers, men and women, especially those in hiring positions, should create equal opportunity hiring to support basic rights and strong companies.

Essay 3

Prompt

As you read the passage below, consider how Graham uses

- ❑ evidence, such as facts or examples, to support claims.

- ❑ reasoning to develop ideas and to connect claims and evidence.

- ❑ stylistic or persuasive elements, such as word choice or appeals to emotion, to add power to the ideas expressed.

Adapted from Renee Graham, "After the Confederate statues come down, then what?" ©2017 by The Boston Globe. Originally published August 22, 2017.

1. From a Robert E. Lee statue at the University of Texas at Austin, to a Jefferson Davis plaque in San Diego, Confederate monuments nationwide are coming down.

2. Of course, this is long overdue, and never should have been necessary in the first place, since men who championed slavery and sedition were never worthy of recognition. Some memorials weren't even hidden behind the false cover of honoring the Confederate dead. In April, New Orleans Mayor Mitch Landrieu, who gave an impassioned speech about the need to eliminate Confederate statues, ordered the removal of four monuments in his city. One was an obelisk erected in 1891 that commemorated a white racist mob's deadly battle against an integrated police force and state militia in 1874. History is supposed to belong to the victors, but for more than a century the descendants of the defeated have choked public spaces with markers of white supremacy.

3. Piece by piece, that is being remedied. Yet once the monuments come down, then what? While doing so is symbolically important, it doesn't begin to address the deeper issues of systemic discrimination that undermine many African-Americans.

4. This recent spate of statue removals was sparked by the murder of Heather Heyer, who died when a car plowed into counter protesters at a racist rally in Charlottesville this month. In a statement about removal of four campus Confederate statues, University of Texas at Austin president Greg Fenves said that Virginia tragedy convinced him "now more than ever, that Confederate monuments have become symbols of modern white supremacy and neo-Nazism."

5. Did Fenves and other officials not recognize that such statues, many erected during the Jim Crow era and the 1960s civil rights movement to intimidate black people, were always symbols of white supremacy? Why wasn't there a similar epiphany when convicted murderer Dylann Roof, trying to start a race war, killed nine African-Americans in their Charleston, S.C., church, in 2015? Only after activist Bree Newsome's

bold action in scaling a pole to remove a Confederate flag on the grounds of South Carolina's State House did officials finally retire the war banner.

6. Taking down such flags and monuments is the least this country can do - and some states don't even want to do that. In May, Alabama passed its Memorial Preservation Act, prohibiting the "relocation, removal, alteration, renaming, or other disturbance of any architecturally significant building, memorial building, memorial street, or monument located on public property" that's more than 40 years old. Defending the law, Alabama's governor, Kay Ivey, said, "When negative aspects of history are repeated, it is often done because we have scrubbed the effects of the past from our memories."

7. That history argument is as phony as a Confederate dollar. Even if every statue, plaque, and monument is removed, it can't erase all the remnants of what Ivey called "our darkest hours" - voter suppression, mass incarceration, racial profiling, and assaults on affirmative action. African-Americans live everyday with "the negative effects" of the same history many fight to preserve.

8. When President Trump asked, "Where does it stop?" in regard to removing Confederate statues, he might as well have been referring to African-American agitation to ensure themselves the same rights and opportunities afforded white Americans. No one will be silenced or pacified because these statues are slowly disappearing. From its first breath when this nation was born, white supremacy has been nimble, always concocting new theories and laws to sustain racial subjugation. Dismantling Confederate imagery is one thing; dismantling the rooted systems of white supremacy they represent won't end with the removal of its metal and marble monuments to racism and treason.

••

Write an essay in which you explain how Graham builds an argument to persuade her audience that removing Confederate statues is not enough in the battle of white supremacy. In your essay, analyze how Graham uses one or more of the features listed above (or features of your own choice) to strengthen the logic and persuasiveness of her argument. Be sure that your analysis focuses on the most relevant features of the passage.

Your essay should not explain whether you agree with Graham's claims, but rather explain how the author builds an argument to persuade her audience.

••

Pre-Essay Writing

Read the essay prompt before you read the provided text. Make sure you have a firm grasp on what the prompt is asking you to analyze in your essay. In this case, the prompt specifically says, "explain how Graham builds an argument to persuade her audience that removing Confederate statues is not enough in the battle of white supremacy". A keyword here is "how". How does Graham persuade her audience? Recall the bullet points already given to you, asking you to notice evidence such as facts, statistics, or reliable experience, reasoning that connects ideas through logic and explanation, and stylistic or persuasive elements such as word choice, emotional appeal, building credibility, etc. Graham's techniques will show up in her body paragraphs. As you read, take note of Graham's use of these things and begin to mentally map out your essay.

Some examples from Graham's text:

Facts

3

a) "In April, New Orleans Mayor Mitch Landrieu, who gave an impassioned speech about the need to eliminate Confederate statues, ordered the removal of four monuments in his city."

b) "This recent spate of statue removals was sparked by the murder of Heather Heyer, who died when a car plowed into counter protesters at a racist rally in Charlottesville this month."

c) "Only after activist Bree Newsome's bold action in scaling a pole to remove a Confederate flag on the grounds of South Carolina's State House did officials finally retire the war banner."

d) "In May, Alabama passed its Memorial Preservation Act, prohibiting the 'relocation, removal, alteration, renaming, or other disturbance of any architecturally significant building, memorial building, memorial street, or monument located on public property' that's more than 40 years old."

Reasoning

a) "History is supposed to belong to the victors..."

b) "Even if every statue, plaque, and monument is removed, it can't erase all the remnants of what Ivey called "our darkest hours" - voter suppression, mass incarceration, racial profiling, and assaults on affirmative action."

c) "African-Americans live everyday with "the negative effects" of the same history many fight to preserve."

d) "From its first breath when this nation was born, white supremacy has been nimble, always concocting new theories and laws to sustain racial subjugation."

Stylistic Elements

a) Rhetorical questions: "Did Fenves and other officials not recognize that such statues, many erected during the Jim Crow era and the 1960s civil rights movement to intimidate black people, were always symbols of white supremacy? Why wasn't there a similar epiphany when convicted murderer Dylann Roof, trying to start a race war, killed nine African-Americans in their Charleston, S.C., church, in 2015?"

b) Strong/definitive word choice: "overdue," "choked," "least," "phony," etc.

d) Words with negative connotations: "racism," "treason," "subjugation," "slavery," etc.

Persuasive Elements

a) **Emotional appeal:** "Why wasn't there a similar epiphany when convicted murderer Dylann Roof, trying to start a race war, killed nine African-Americans in their Charleston, S.C., church, in 2015?"

b) **Counterclaim:** "That history argument is as phony as a Confederate dollar. Even if every statue, plaque, and monument is removed, it can't erase all the remnants of what Ivey called "our darkest hours" — voter suppression, mass incarceration, racial profiling, and assaults on affirmative action."

d) **Credibility (built with example after example):** University of Texas at Austin, San Diego, New Orleans, Alabama, Charleston.

Thoroughly read through the entire text given, paying special attention to key points. You will only have time for one full read through. Key points will be quickly exposed through a thesis-like statement and topic sentences. An author's thesis statement most often appears in the introductory paragraph, though Graham's can be found after some short background.

Graham's Thesis:

Yet once the monuments come down, then what? While doing so is symbolically important, it doesn't begin to address the deeper issues of systemic discrimination that undermine many African-Americans.

Graham's Topic sentences:

Topic sentences are the first sentence of every paragraph.

"Of course, this is long overdue, and never should have been necessary in the first place, since men who championed slavery and sedition were never worthy of recognition."

"This recent spate of statue removals was sparked by the murder of Heather Heyer, who died when a car plowed into counter protesters at a racist rally in Charlottesville this month."

"Taking down such flags and monuments is the least this country can do — and some states don't even want to do that."

"That history argument is as phony as a Confederate dollar."

"When President Trump asked, "Where does it stop?" in regard to removing Confederate statues, he might as well have been referring to African-American agitation to ensure themselves the same rights and opportunities afforded white Americans."

Etc.

The author's key points will be the structure that your own key points mimic. In this case, Graham's key points are a racist past that still exists, some people's denial, and a need to face racism more aggressively. Analyze these points for persuasive techniques, and you have strong word choice, rhetorical questions, and a counterclaim. These three things are the "how" that the sample essay chooses to focus on, but Graham uses other techniques (like those examples given above), as well, to persuade her audience. No two essays will be alike as you and your peers will analyze Graham's work through a personal lens.

Create a clear and concise thesis that states the author's persuasive techniques.

Sample essay's thesis: *She works to persuade a U.S. audience of this by using strong word choice, asking rhetorical questions, and addressing statue supporters in a direct counterclaim.*

For detailed analysis, these techniques could reasonably be a list of 2-4 (3, in the sample essay's case). One essay style is to focus each body paragraph on one of those techniques. Another style would be to summarize like techniques in paragraphs together. Paraphrase and quote a few specific lines from the text that support your analysis. Keep any quotes used relatively short. Make sure to always surround a quote with your own words. Introduce the quote, include the quote, and then clearly explain why this quote shows the author's persuasive technique. The essay should be mostly your words, not the authors.

Conclude your essay by pointing out the author's intentions, along with their specific audience. Avoid merely restating your thesis.

Sample essay: *Even though statue removal is an important and necessary step in fighting white supremacy and neo-Nazism, citizens and officials need to recognize that it is just a start. When American society is so deeply-rooted in racism, removal of a few faces won't cure dangerous mindsets overnight. Graham persuades the reader that much more needs to be done in order for the American nation and its people to be healthy.*

Answer Sheet

Use a No. 2 pencil. Begin your essay on this page. If you need more space, continue on the next page.

_____

_____

_____

_____

_____

_____

_____

_____

_____

3

Sample Essay

3

In an effort to stop encouraging white supremacy, statues of men who historically represent the Confederacy and its racism are being brought down across the United States. Renee Graham argues that, while this removal of Confederate statues is important, it doesn't do enough to eradicate America of its racism. She works to persuade a U.S. audience of this by using definitive word choice, asking rhetorical questions, and addressing statue supporters in a direct counterclaim.

Graham chooses her words wisely as she describes the past and present state of racial upheaval in the U.S. While some citizens are opposed to the small effort of Confederate statue removal, Graham claims the act is "long overdue" and these reminders of white supremacy have "choked public spaces" for too long. Definitive words like "over due" and "choked" ring with an authoritative tone. Graham continues to use strong, definitive words when she states that the statue removal is merely "the least" we could do to combat our racism. "Least" points out that taking away a face of the Confederacy is almost nothing when it comes up against ingrained subjugation. There's so much more that needs to be done, especially when you take into account the "nimble" nature of white supremacy. Graham uses "nimble" to remind the audience of the true craftiness white supremacy uses in order to stick around for hundreds of years.

Speaking of sticking around, Graham draws her audience in further by directly asking them questions about how these statues have gotten to stay in our nation. She asks rhetorical questions, questions meant for the audience to contemplate but not necessarily answer. For example, when a college president, Fenves, was quoted saying that the Confederate monuments are increasing symbols of neo-Nazism, Graham asks the reader how he and other officials have not realized that "many [statues] erected during the Jim Crow era and the 1960s civil rights movement to intimidate black people, were always symbols of white supremacy?" She asks the reader this rhetorical question because it should be clear that the symbolism of these people has always been offensive. In another instance, she asks the reader why there wasn't "a similar epiphany" when Dylann Roof killed nine African Americans in 2015. Again, she asks these questions to show the sticking nature of white supremacy, pointing out that these statues have been around for forever because these mindsets and prejudices have been/are around for forever. Graham aims for her audience of citizens and officials to realize that removing statues will not be enough and may not mean anything at all in the battle against white supremacy.

Lastly, Graham directly discredits those who oppose the simple removal of Confederate statues. The governor of Alabama, Kay Ivey, claimed that negative aspects of society continue because we have "scrubbed the effects" from our collective memories; therefore, statues should be kept. Graham tears a hole in this logic when she counterclaims that removing every monument, statue, etc. could never get rid of all remnants of a racist past as "voter suppression, mass incarceration, racial profiling, and assaults on affirmative action" are still a very real thing. This reminds the audience that all of these realities are lived with on a daily basis which African-Americans are not likely to forget. Again, as Donald Trump asks, "Where does it stop?" in reference to statue removal, Graham answers. She reminds the audience that no one will be truly pacified by missing statues and taking greater measures will also not strip the past from our memories. The Confederacy is just a small piece of a deep-seated prejudice, after all.

Graham persuades the reader that much more needs to be done in order for the American nation and its people to be healthy. Her word choice, rhetorical questions, and counterclaim all work against naysayer logic to remind the reader that American society is so deeply-rooted in racism, removal of a few faces won't cure dangerous mindsets overnight. Moreover, statue removal is just a start.

3

Essay 4

Prompt

As you read the passage below, consider how Upton uses

❑ evidence, such as facts or examples, to support claims.

❑ reasoning to develop ideas and to connect claims and evidence.

❑ stylistic or persuasive elements, such as word choice or appeals to emotion, to add power to the ideas expressed.

Adapted from John Kirby, "Stop the politics and honor the fallen" ©2017 by CNN. Originally published October 18, 2017.

1. The bickering over President Trump's phone call to the grieving widow of Army Sgt. La David Johnson needs to stop.

2. Put aside for a moment that Mr. Trump didn't acknowledge for more than a week the deaths of four American soldiers fighting ISIS in Niger. Put aside for a moment that he publicized the fact he would be making calls and sending letters. Put aside, even, that in the midst of one of those calls, he may have made an insensitive remark regarding what Sgt. Johnson knew "he signed up for."

3. Put all that aside ... just for a moment. And focus on Myeshia Johnson, her family and, most especially, her children. Take one long look at the images of that young woman collapsed across the flag-draped casket of her equally young husband and tell me how in the hell you can justify politicizing this tragedy.

4. There are two bright, beautiful kids right now - 6-year-old Ah'leeysa and toddler Ladavid Johnson Jr. - who will never see their father again, never feel his warm embrace, never sit atop his shoulders, never hear him say how much he loves them.

5. Ah'leeysa may one day be comforted by memories of her daddy, but it's doubtful little Ladavid Jr. will. And then there is the Johnson's unborn child, who will never know his or her soldier father.

6. You can be sure the Army is wrapping its arms around this family, as it will the other three families so devastated by the outcome of this dangerous mission in Niger - those of Staff Sgt. Bryan Black, Staff Sgt. Jeremiah Johnson and Staff Sgt. Dustin Wright.

7. These families deserve our respect, our sympathy, our quiet gratitude. More critically, they deserve the time and space to deal with the unspeakable grief and sorrow they now endure, as well as every ounce of support that can be mustered to help them through it.

8. Those of us left untouched by this kind of loss are in no position to judge or even comprehend how they will best do this. We may stake no claim to representing, advocating or otherwise holding forth about the grieving process. There are experts, clergy and loved ones who can manage this far better than the rest of us.

9. But we can, and we should, as a nation, endeavor to honor and help comfort the families of the fallen. And that includes our commander in chief. Indeed, he more than any other.

10. His job, when required, is to send men and women into harm's way. And should those men and women not survive the mission, his other job is to make sure they return home in a dignified, professional manner to families that will experience not only our gratitude but our unconditional support. President George W. Bush referred to this as being the "Comforter-in-Chief," and it's probably the most important duty any occupier of the Oval Office obeys.

11. Mr. Trump has been derelict in that duty today.

12. Does it matter whether or not the President said something that offended Mrs. Johnson? Absolutely it does. And if he did, he ought to be man enough to admit it and apologize. As a matter of fact, regardless of what he said, he should still apologize to the members of the Johnson family, who are now, sadly, a Gold Star family. And one of those family members - Sgt. Johnson's mother - backed up Democratic Congresswoman Frederica Wilson's claim that the conversation upset Myeisha.

13. That should be all the "proof" Mr. Trump needs.

14. Such an apology is likely not forthcoming. So, the next best thing he - and quite frankly everyone else, including Rep. Wilson - should do, is stop. Stop making it worse. Stop throwing barbs and rejoinders. Stop turning this into a political fight and focus instead on doing what must be done to honor the sacrifices these four men made.

15. If there's one thing - one damn thing, for goodness sake - we should all be able to agree on, it's our responsibility to show respect for the families of our fallen troops.

16. White House press secretary Sarah Sanders told reporters Wednesday that White House chief of staff John Kelly is "disgusted by the way this has been politicized and that the focus has come on the process and not the fact that American lives were lost."

17. Kelly is right, of course. He knows all too well the pain the Johnsons and the Blacks and the Wrights and the Johnsons are feeling right now. Nobody so close to Trump is more credible on the issue.

18. Here's hoping he made those same points to his boss.

Write an essay in which you explain how Kirby builds an argument to persuade his audience that when soldier's lives are lost, we should honor them and drop the politics. In your essay, analyze how Kirby uses one or more of the features listed above (or features of your own choice) to strengthen the logic and persuasiveness of his argument. Be sure that your analysis focuses on the most relevant features of the passage.

Your essay should not explain whether you agree with Kirby's claims, but rather explain how the author builds an argument to persuade his audience.

4

Pre-Essay Writing

Read the essay prompt before you read the provided text. Make sure you have a firm grasp on what the prompt is asking you to analyze in your essay. In this case, the prompt specifically says, "explain how Kirby builds an argument to persuade his audience that when soldier's lives are lost, we should honor them and drop the politics". A keyword here is "how". How does Kirby persuade his audience? Recall the bullet points already given to you, asking you to notice evidence such as facts, statistics, or reliable experience, reasoning that connects ideas through logic and explanation, and stylistic or persuasive elements such as word choice, emotional appeal, building credibility, etc. Kirby's techniques will show up in his body paragraphs. As you read, take note of Kirby's use of these things and begin to mentally map out your essay.

Some examples from Kirby's text:

Facts

a) "There are two bright, beautiful kids right now - 6-year-old Ah'leeysa and toddler Ladavid Johnson Jr. - who will never see their father again, never feel his warm embrace, never sit atop his shoulders, never hear him say how much he loves them."

b) "There are experts, clergy and loved ones who can manage this far better than the rest of us."

c) "You can be sure the Army is wrapping its arms around this family, as it will the other three families so devastated by the outcome of this dangerous mission in Niger - those of Staff Sgt. Bryan Black, Staff Sgt. Jeremiah Johnson and Staff Sgt. Dustin Wright."

d) "White House press secretary Sarah Sanders told reporters Wednesday that White House chief of staff John Kelly is "disgusted by the way this has been politicized and that the focus has come on the process and not the fact that American lives were lost.""

Reasoning

a) "Take one long look at the images of that young woman collapsed across the flag-draped casket of her equally young husband and tell me how in the hell you can justify politicizing this tragedy."

b) "More critically, they deserve the time and space to deal with the unspeakable grief and sorrow they now endure, as well as every ounce of support that can be mustered to help them through it."

c) "Those of us left untouched by this kind of loss are in no position to judge or even comprehend how they will best do this."

d) "Does it matter whether or not the President said something that offended Mrs. Johnson? Absolutely it does."

Stylistic Elements

a) **Repetition:** Put aside for a moment that Mr. Trump didn't acknowledge for more than a week the deaths of four American soldiers fighting ISIS in Niger. Put aside for a moment that he publicized the fact he would be making calls and sending letters. Put aside, even, that in the midst of one of those calls, he may have made an insensitive remark regarding what Sgt. Johnson knew "he signed up for." Etc.

b) **Passionate word choice:** "how in the hell," "one damn thing," etc.

c) **Incomplete sentences:** "But we can, and we should, as a nation, endeavor to honor and help comfort the families of the fallen. And that includes our commander in chief. Indeed, he more than any other." Etc.

Persuasive Elements

a) **Emotional appeal:** "There are two bright, beautiful kids right now - 6-year-old Ah'leeysa and toddler Ladavid Johnson Jr. - who will never see their father again, never feel his warm embrace, never sit atop his shoulders, never hear him say how much he loves them." Etc.

b) **Counterclaim:** "Such an apology is likely not forthcoming. So, the next best thing he - and quite frankly everyone else, including Rep. Wilson - should do, is stop. Stop making it worse."

c) **Credibility:** "Put aside for a moment that Mr. Trump didn't acknowledge for more than a week the deaths of four American soldiers fighting ISIS in Niger. Put aside for a moment that he publicized the fact he would be making calls and sending letters. Put aside, even, that in the midst of one of those calls, he may have made an insensitive remark regarding what Sgt. Johnson knew "he signed up for." Etc.

Thoroughly read through the entire text given, paying special attention to key points. You will only have time for one full read through. Key points will be quickly exposed through a thesis-like statement and topic sentences. An author's thesis statement most often appears in the introductory paragraph and/or title. Kirby's thesis is in the title, in the first line of the article, and reinforced throughout.

Kirby's Thesis:

The bickering over President Trump's phone call to the grieving widow of Army Sgt. La David Johnson needs to stop.

Kirby's Topic sentences:

Topic sentences are the first sentence of every paragraph.

"Put aside for a moment that Mr. Trump didn't acknowledge for more than a week the deaths of four American soldiers fighting ISIS in Niger."

"These families deserve our respect, our sympathy, our quiet gratitude."

"His job, when required, is to send men and women into harm's way."

"Does it matter whether or not the President said something that offended Mrs. Johnson?"

Etc.

The author's key points will be the structure that your own key points mimic. In this case, Kirby's key points are recent awful events, the effects of these events on family, the effect these events should have on everyone. Analyze these points for supported examples, purposeful stylistic choices, and emotional appeals. These three things are the "how" that the sample essay chooses to focus on, but Kirby uses other techniques (like those examples given above), as well, to persuade his audience. No two essays will be alike as you and your peers will analyze Kirby's work through a personal lens.

Create a clear and concise thesis that states the author's persuasive techniques.

Sample essay's thesis: *He supports his claim by approaching examples in a variety of ways, making purposeful syntax and diction choices, and appealing to audience emotions.*

For detailed analysis, these techniques could reasonably be a list of 2-4 (3, in the sample essay's case). One essay style is to focus each body paragraph on one of those techniques. Another style would be to summarize like techniques in paragraphs together. Paraphrase and quote a few specific lines from the text that support your analysis. Keep any quotes used relatively short. Make sure to always surround a quote with your own words. Introduce the quote, include the quote, and then clearly explain why this quote shows the author's persuasive technique. The essay should be mostly your words, not the authors.

Conclude your essay by pointing out the author's intentions, along with their specific audience. Avoid merely restating your thesis.

Sample essay: *It's easy to get wrapped up in the political debate that surrounds President Trump and the decisions he has made here. Kirby knows this, for sure. However, the four soldiers and their families deserve respect, honor, and memory. At another time, in a different platform, readers can turn political, but for now, politics need to drop. Kirby aims to get his readers to see, hear, and feel the truth of this.*

Answer Sheet

Use a No. 2 pencil. Begin your essay on this page. If you need more space, continue on the next page.

4

4

Sample Essay

There's a time and a place for everything. At least, that's what they say. And that's exactly how John Kirby, writer for CNN, feels about the recent political upheaval after President Trump treated four soldier's deaths insensitively. Kirby claims that when soldiers have lost their lives, we should honor them and drop the politics. He supports his claim by approaching examples in a variety of ways, making purposeful syntax and diction choices, and appealing to audience emotions.

Kirby uses one specific example, the recent death of four soldiers in Niger, but he approaches the example in a variety of ways, bringing the wrongful focus on politics to light. Kirby first uses names. The four soldiers are: Army Sgt. La David Johnson, Staff Sgt. Bryan Black, Staff Sgt. Jeremiah Johnson and Staff Sgt. Dustin Wright. Kirby makes sure to say the names of these men to make them real to the reader. It's a reminder that they were indeed real people, with impressive titles, even. Kirby also uses logic. He explains that those of us who are untouched by an incredible public loss like this can't even comprehend how it is/will affect family members. Because of this, we should put our emphasis on respect and honor. It's logic like this that Kirby aims to grab the reader with. Kirby calls upon the words of two others in correlation with this example, as well. He quotes George W. Bush and his encouragement for the president to be a "Comforter-in-Chief," and he quotes John Kelly who echoes Kirby's sentiments about focusing on lost lives. These quotations are used to add more voices in support of Kirby's claim, building the argument despite only using one example.

Kirby uses unique stylistic choices in his writing with both syntax and diction to emphasize his point. He utilizes repetition with the phrase "Put aside". Kirby's repetition of this phrase specifically encourages the reader to forget about the disappointment in politics at the moment and be emotionally connected to the issue. He does this again with his repetition of the word "never", an ugly reminder to the reader that children lost their father. He adds in another unique stylistic choice with his use of incomplete sentences. With many sentences starting with "And" and "But," there is a stronger sense that the author has a long list of support. Lastly, Kirby makes sure to step away from the professional for a moment, inserting passionate words into the situation. He states "how in the hell" can you be political when a family is in mourning, and "one damn thing" we should all support doing is being respectful. Kirby uses these passionate words like a father, scolding his child. He aims to snap the reader into realizing the foolishness of losing themselves in politics instead of the tragedy.

The article is saturated with Kirby's attempts to appeal to the reader's emotions, reminding everyone of the sad reality of these deaths and the sad reality of everyone's reactions. When Kirby repeatedly tells everyone to "put aside" what has happened with Pres. Trump, he simultaneously acknowledges the error of the events. He seems to say, "Yes, what the President did was bad, but…" This early acknowledgement validates any political anger the reader may have, building his credibility and showing his level-headed understanding of both sides. Along a similar vein, Kirby brings up Trump and his foibles again at the end of the article. He states that Trump should apologize but he mostly likely won't, so what do we do in the meantime? Stop making it worse. Kirby's approach is almost like a counterclaim, anticipating a reader's disagreement, but quelling it before it begins. The most gutting emotional appeals are all of Kirby's references to Army Sgt. La David Johnson's family. His wife laying on the coffin. His children struggling to remember their dad. All of these things aim to tug on the heartstrings of the reader, reminding them to put the soldiers' families first.

It's easy to get wrapped up in the political debate that surrounds President Trump and the decisions he has made here. Kirby knows this, for sure. However, the four soldiers and their families deserve respect, honor, and memory. At another time, in a different platform, readers can turn political, but for now, politics need to drop. Kirby aims to get his readers to see, hear, and feel the truth of this.

4

Essay 5

Prompt

As you read the passage below, consider how Cywinski uses

❑ evidence, such as facts or examples, to support claims.

❑ reasoning to develop ideas and to connect claims and evidence.

❑ stylistic or persuasive elements, such as word choice or appeals to emotion, to add power to the ideas expressed.

Adapted from Piotr M.A. Cywinski, "In the face of hatred, we cannot be indifferent" ©2017 by CNN. Originally published August 18, 2017.

1. Barely seven decades ago, smoke billowed from the chimneys of the Auschwitz-Birkenau crematoria. They smoked incessantly because the German Nazis wanted to completely exterminate European Jews.

2. The Holocaust - the Shoah - did not come out of nowhere.

3. The Auschwitz concentration camp was established before the extermination camp came into being. Prior to that, Polish territories were occupied and incorporated into the Third Reich. Sometime earlier still, the Second World War broke out across Europe. Before the war, Jews were deprived of fundamental rights and civil liberties in Germany. And before that, Adolf Hitler and his National Socialist German Workers' Party - the Nazis - won in democratic, free elections.

4. We have seen similar kinds of hatred pop up in numerous guises throughout history - before and after the Holocaust. The model, however, is always more or less the same.

5. First, social frustration provides fertile ground to demagogy and populism. Then, the absence of an early response blurs the boundary of acceptable public discourse and the hate speech intensifies -- followed by acts of hate. The imagined enemy - the scapegoat - is then dehumanized. Finally, it turns out to be too late. The machine of institutionalized hatred does away with any form of social control.

6. It happened in the very heart of Europe. It happened in Rwanda. It was what the Armenians experienced. It all happened so recently that it is still contemporary history.

7. And today, in Europe, in the US and many other democratic countries, neo-Nazis, racists, anti-Semites, nationalists and xenophobes are reviving and growing in strength.

8. Under the pretext of freedom of speech and the right to public expression of views - values which mean nothing to them - preachers of hatred are once again poisoning people's minds. Their slogans appear in the

media and they are increasingly represented at the polls. It's all as if nothing had happened.

9. Primo Levi, a Holocaust survivor, warned: "It happened, therefore it can happen again ... It can happen anywhere."

10. A similar fear is expressed in the words of all those who experienced the hell of Auschwitz. Those whose hope rests in two words: "never again." Devastatingly, they lived to witness the fragility of this call.

11. Today, only a few of those witnesses are still alive - right at the moment the Hydra of hatred is beginning to re grow the brown-shirted monster's head.

12. This raises an alarming question about the awareness and responsibility of politicians, journalists, educators, historians and people like me.

13. The choice is simple: either we collectively put forward a clear and absolute stop to hate speech and acts of hate. Or we will walk down the path of indifference. The latter option, however, only leads to acquiescence to evil. It will only bring us closer to human suffering and death.

14. On the 70th anniversary of the liberation of Auschwitz, Ronald Lauder - the man who publicly refused to shake hands with Austrian President Kurt Waldheim, a former Nazi - said: "World silence leads to Auschwitz. World indifference leads to Auschwitz."

15. I believe he was right. Freedom, democracy, human rights, justice. These are not values given once and for all. We quickly forget about them and treat them as a definitive acquisition of civilization.

16. Now would be a good time for us to remember words of Elie Wiesel, who warned: "indifference is the epitome of evil."

17. We stand at a crossroads. This is the moment - perhaps the last moment - when people in free countries can still choose how to shape our educational system, public debate and the language we use in our political discourse.

18. Either we grasp this opportunity and reject this hatred. Or, we choose to remain indifferent.

Write an essay in which you explain how Cywinski builds an argument to persuade his audience that intense hatred is in resurgence and action needs to be taken against it. In your essay, analyze how Cywinski uses one or more of the features listed above (or features of your own choice) to strengthen the logic and persuasiveness of his argument. Be sure that your analysis focuses on the most relevant aspects of the passage.

Your essay should not explain whether you agree with Cywinski's claims, but rather explain how the author builds an argument to persuade his audience.

Pre-Essay Writing

Read the essay prompt before you read the provided text. Make sure you have a firm grasp on what the prompt is asking you to analyze in your essay. In this case, the prompt specifically says, "explain how Cywinski builds an argument to persuade his audience that intense hatred is in resurgence and action needs to be taken against it". A keyword here is "how". How does Cywinski persuade his audience? Recall the bullet points already given to you, asking you to notice evidence such as facts, statistics, or reliable experience, reasoning that connects ideas through logic and explanation, and stylistic or persuasive elements such as word choice, emotional appeal, building credibility, etc. Cywinski's techniques will show up in his body paragraphs. As you read, take note of Cywinski's use of these things and begin to mentally map out your essay.

Some examples from Cywinski's text:

Facts

   a) "Barely seven decades ago, smoke billowed from the chimneys of the Auschwitz-Birkenau crematoria."

   b) "The Auschwitz concentration camp was established before the extermination camp came into being."

   c) "Before the war, Jews were deprived of fundamental rights and civil liberties in Germany."

   d) "It happened in the very heart of Europe. It happened in Rwanda. It was what the Armenians experienced.

Reasoning

   a) "The Holocaust - the Shoah - did not come out of nowhere."

   b) "We have seen similar kinds of hatred pop up in numerous guises throughout history - before and after the Holocaust. The model, however, is always more or less the same."

c) "Under the pretext of freedom of speech and the right to public expression of views - values which mean nothing to them - preachers of hatred are once again poisoning people's minds."

d) "The choice is simple: either we collectively put forward a clear and absolute stop to hate speech and acts of hate. Or we will walk down the path of indifference."

Stylistic Elements

a) **Descriptive word choice:** "billowed," "fertile ground," "model," "Hydra of hatred," etc.

b) **Strong word choice:** "demagogy," "populism," "institutionalized hatred," "poisoning," etc.

c) **Fragments:** "Either we grasp this opportunity and reject this hatred. Or, we choose to remain indifferent." "Freedom, democracy, human rights, justice."

Persuasive Elements

a) **Ultimatum:** "The choice is simple: either we collectively put forward a clear and absolute stop to hate speech and acts of hate. Or we will walk down the path of indifference. The latter option, however, only leads to acquiescence to evil. It will only bring us closer to human suffering and death." "This is the moment - perhaps the last moment"

b) **Compare past and present:** "We have seen similar kinds of hatred pop up in numerous guises throughout history - before and after the Holocaust. The model, however, is always more or less the same... And today, in Europe, in the US and many other democratic countries, neo-Nazis, racists, anti-Semites, nationalists and xenophobes are reviving and growing in strength."

c) **Credibility:** Primo Levi, a Holocaust survivor, warned: "It happened, therefore it can happen again ... It can happen anywhere." "Now would be a good time for us to remember words of Elie Wiesel, who warned: 'indifference is the epitome of evil.'"

Thoroughly read through the entire text given, paying special attention to key points. You will only have time for one full read through. Key points will be quickly exposed through a thesis-like statement and topic sentences. An author's thesis statement most often appears in the introductory paragraph and can be hinted at in the title. Cywinski's thesis is clear in the title (In the face of hatred, we cannot be indifferent), and he implies his opinion towards acting against hate all the way up to the end.

Cywinski's Thesis:

And today, in Europe, in the US and many other democratic countries, neo-Nazis, racists, anti-Semites, nationalists and xenophobes are reviving and growing in strength...Either we grasp this opportunity and reject this hatred. Or, we choose to remain indifferent.

Cywinski's Topic sentences:

Topic sentences are the first sentence of every paragraph.

"The Holocaust - the Shoah - did not come out of nowhere."

"We have seen similar kinds of hatred pop up in numerous guises throughout history - before and after the Holocaust."

"Under the pretext of freedom of speech and the right to public expression of views - values which mean nothing to them -- preachers of hatred are once again poisoning people's minds."

"Primo Levi, a Holocaust survivor, warned: 'It happened, therefore it can happen again ... It can happen anywhere.'"

Etc.

The author's key points will be the structure that your own key points mimic. In this case, Cywinski's key points are the pattern of institutionalized hatred, the rise in hatred today, and the need to act against it. Analyze these points for persuasive techniques, and you have descriptive word choice, comparing the past to the present, and credibility. These three things are the "how" that the sample essay chooses to focus on, but Cywinski uses other techniques (like those examples given above), as well, to persuade his audience. Remember, no two essays will be alike as you and your peers will analyze Cywinski's work through a personal lens.

Create a clear and concise thesis that states the author's persuasive techniques.

Sample essay's thesis: *He supports his claim by using descriptive word choice, comparing the past to the present, and quoting credible voices.*

For detailed analysis, these techniques could reasonably be a list of 2-4 (3, in the sample essay's case). One essay style is to focus each body paragraph on one of those techniques. Another style would be to summarize like techniques in paragraphs together. Paraphrase and quote a few specific lines from the text that support your analysis. Keep any quotes used relatively short. Make sure to always surround a quote with your own words. Introduce the quote, include the quote, and then clearly explain why this quote shows the author's persuasive technique. The essay should be mostly your words, not the author's.

Conclude your essay by pointing out the author's intentions, along with their specific audience. Avoid merely restating your thesis.

Sample essay: *No one believes that hate is absent from the earth, but it's difficult for people to remember that large scale hate, holocaust scale hate, is still possible, too. Cywinski works to persuade anyone who will listen that indifference will be the catalyst bringing society right back through that ugly process. He pleads for us to take the opportunity we have now to actually act.*

Answer Sheet

Use a No. 2 pencil. Begin your essay on this page. If you need more space, continue on the next page.

5

5

Sample Essay

Hatred is an ugly human attribute that has shown up on the earth in devastating degrees. As humans move forward, one would think that lessons are learned, and hatred is lost. M.A. Cywinski, though, in his article for CNN, claims that intense hatred is actually in resurgence, and citizens, politicians, educators, etc., must act to stop it. He supports his claim by using descriptive word choice, comparing the past to the present, and quoting credible voices.

Cywinksi chooses his words wisely to revive any lost feelings of shock and remorse in the reader. When he opens his argument by recalling devastating deaths in Auschwitz, he uses words like "billowed" and "incessantly" to describe the smoke. These descriptors bring back a disturbing image of the holocaust, an image that won't allow the reader to forget the power of hate. Cywinksi then refers to the societal process of the holocaust as a "model". Referring to the holocaust as a model, gives the reader an unsettling thought that such a heinous event was and is not a standalone. Could it be true that such hate continues? At times, there's hope that another Auschwitz will never happen, but Cywinksi reminds his audience of the "fragility" of this calm. Just like that, with his unique word choice, he denies his audience the chance to forget about large scale hatred and its relevance to today.

Cywinski also links the devastating acts of the past to the present, in an effort to make a hate resurgence seem real. The holocaust only seems far removed from today, for the societal process that lead to it has actually been repeated time and time again. Cywinski reviews this process; societal frustration leads to demagogy, which leads to hate speech, which leads to acts of hate, which dehumanizes the enemy, and results in "institutionalized" hatred. With the breakdown of this process, Cywinski shows the reader how logical and easy it is to go down this path again. He continues with further examples. "It happened in the very heart of Europe. It happened in Rwanda. It was what the Armenians experienced." Cywinksi gives his reader clear examples of mankind repeating the hate witnessed in Germany. His last example is the most relatable, though; "And today, in Europe, in the US and many other democratic countries, neo-Nazis, racists, anti-Semites, nationalists and xenophobes are reviving and growing in strength." By linking the hate groups of the present to the hate groups of the past, Cywinski reminds the audience to recognize just how close we are to repeating devastating hatred again.

If Cywinski's description and logic wasn't enough to incite belief and action in his audience, he hopes the words of first-hand hate survivors will. Cywinski quotes Primo Levi, a holocaust survivor that warned if such an event can happen once, it can happen again. Cywinski uses this credible voice to persuade his audience of hate's imminent presence, especially if nothing is done. He motivates further by quoting one man, Ronald Lauder, who took a stand by not shaking the hand of a former Nazi; "World silence leads to Auschwitz. World indifference leads to Auschwitz." Silence will not rid the world of its problems. Cywinksi calls on one last credible and well-known voice, Elie Wiesel, who said that "indifference is the epitome of evil." Harsh words for people to hear, but words that citizens, politicians, and everyone, according to Cywinski, needs to hear in order to act.

Cywinski works to persuade anyone who will listen that indifference will be the catalyst bringing society right back through that ugly process. His descriptive words remind the audience of an ugly past. His breakdown of links between the past and present make hatred more present, and his quotes from hatred survivors bring credibility to his argument. He pleads for us to take the opportunity we have now to actually act.

Essay 6

Prompt

As you read the passage below, consider how Upton uses

❏ evidence, such as facts or examples, to support claims.

❏ reasoning to develop ideas and to connect claims and evidence.

❏ stylistic or persuasive elements, such as word choice or appeals to emotion, to add power to the ideas expressed.

Adapted from Ben Sin, "Do Not Buy The Lazy Rehash That is Apple's iPhone 8" ©2017 by Forbes. Originally published September 13, 2017.

1. Unless you have avoided the internet for the past eight hours and this is the first piece you're reading (in which case, thanks!), you have very likely heard about and seen pictures of Apple's new iPhones. After all, the annual iPhone announcement is such a pop culture phenomenon that every publication, even ones which do not cover tech traditionally, suddenly become "smart phone experts" during this 24-hour period.

2. While the iPhone X (pronounced "iPhone 10") is every bit as impressive as all the leaks and rumors have long suggested, Apple also introduced two other iPhones - dubbed the 8 and 8 Plus - that are in my opinion complete lazy rehashes.

3. From the second gen iPhone (the 3G) to the iPhone 6S (a period from 2008 to 2016), Apple had followed a two-year cycle for design updates. That meant Apple would change how the device looked every two years, with the "no-change" year models given the "S" signifier. This is honest marketing/advertising on Apple's part, because the improvements in the S devices were often so minor - (do you remember the difference between the iPhone 6S and the 6, or the 3GS and the 3G?) - it would be disingenuous to market it as an entirely new iPhone with a numerical jump.

4. (Those who are familiar with video games may remember Cap com taking this approach in the '90s when it released like five Street Fighter II variants before jumping to III.)

5. Last year's iPhone 7 broke that trend by keeping the same overall look of the iPhone 6 and 6S. It was the first iPhone to "go up a number" while keeping the overall physical design essentially the same. Many tech writers (including myself) pointed out that the design was a bit dated and boring.

6. So, imagine what we're thinking now that Apple has officially confirmed it's keeping the 2014 design of the iPhone 6 for a fourth straight year with the iPhone 8.

7. Reporters (not columnists, like myself) have to report the iPhone 8's launch straight, but you can almost

feel how bored they are with the 8 by the lack of coverage. On the homepages of traditional tech sites like CNET, PC Mag, Wired, a photo and headline about the iPhone X dominates the landing page, while the iPhone 8 is nowhere to be found - you'd have to scroll down to see coverage. And rightfully so. The iPhone 8, in my opinion, is so bland, it deserves this type of "oh yeah by the way" coverage.

8. I am aware that the iPhone 8 has a few tricks up its sleeves over the iPhone 7, such as wireless charging (a feature that Samsung has been offering for like four years); a "True Tone" display (I tested the new iPad Pro 10.5 with this feature alongside my own older iPad Pro, and I could barely tell the difference); and some artificial lighting when taking portraits. That's it. The camera hardware is exactly the same, as is the display resolution.

9. The bezels around the iPhone 6/7/8 were laughably large in 2017 already, going into 2018? What excuse is there for Apple to not at least trim the iPhone 8's bezels a bit? I have $160 phones on me right now from unknown Chinese companies that make the iPhone 8's physical design look old.

10. Some of you may think I'm being superficial, dwelling on the recycled appearance this much. But that's the whole point of being a gadget geek/techie, right? Companies pump out new updates to phones every year mostly to appeal to our eyes - we all know deep down that a Samsung Galaxy S7 can do virtually the exact same thing the Galaxy S8 does. We just want the S8 because it looks so, so much cooler. Your day to day phone usage isn't going to change if you switch from the iPhone 7 to the 8.

11. In fact, the iPhone 8 annoys me so much - I'm not even going to review it. Apple's PR told me I will likely have to wait quite a while to get to test the iPhone X, while the iPhone 8 review units will open up a lot sooner. But that's fine, I'll wait however long to test the iPhone X, the only new Apple device worth acknowledging. I'm not giving the 8 any more attention after this post.

12. I suggest readers do the same. The iPhone X may be pricey, but if you must buy a new Apple phone anytime in the next year, go for the X, or buy the iPhone 7 for a discount. Do not buy the iPhone 8 -- it's not worth it.

13. I'll let this tweet [@JarrodAlonge: The iPhone X is the actual iPhone 8. The 8 only exists to justify the X being $1,000. Just buy a refurbished iPhone 6 for $200, you chumps.] conclude my thoughts.

••

Write an essay in which you explain how Sin builds an argument to persuade his audience that they should not buy the iPhone 8. In your essay, analyze how Sin uses one or more of the features listed above (or features of your own choice) to strengthen the logic and persuasiveness of his argument. Be sure that your analysis focuses on the most relevant features of the passage.

Your essay should not explain whether you agree with Sin's claims, but rather explain how the author builds an argument to persuade his audience.

••

Pre-Essay Writing

Read the essay prompt before you read the provided text. Make sure you have a firm grasp on what the prompt is asking you to analyze in your essay. In this case, the prompt specifically says, "explain how Sin builds an argument to persuade his audience that they should not buy the iPhone 8". A keyword here is "how". How does Sin persuade his audience? Recall the bullet points already given to you, asking you to notice evidence such as facts, statistics, or reliable experience, reasoning that connects ideas through logic and explanation, and stylistic or persuasive elements such as word choice, emotional appeal, building credibility, etc. Sin's techniques will show up in his body paragraphs. As you read, take note of Sin's use of these things and begin to mentally map out your essay.

Some examples from Sin's text:

Facts

  a) "From the second gen iPhone (the 3G) to the iPhone 6S (a period from 2008 to 2016), Apple had followed a two-year cycle for design updates."

  b) "Last year's iPhone 7 broke that trend by keeping the same overall look of the iPhone 6 and 6S."

  c) "That meant Apple would change how the device looked every two years, with the "no-change" year models given the "S" signifier."

  d) "Apple's PR told me I will likely have to wait quite a while to get to test the iPhone X, while the iPhone 8 review units will open up a lot sooner."

Reasoning

  a) "After all, the annual iPhone announcement is such a pop culture phenomenon that every publication, even ones which do not cover tech traditionally, suddenly become "smartphone experts" during this 24-hour period."

b) "So, imagine what we're thinking now that Apple has officially confirmed it's keeping the 2014 design of the iPhone 6 for a fourth straight year with the iPhone 8."

c) "Reporters (not columnists, like myself) have to report the iPhone 8's launch straight, but you can almost feel how bored they are with the 8 by the lack of coverage."

d) "What excuse is there for Apple to not at least trim the iPhone 8's bezels a bit? I have $160 phones on me right now from unknown Chinese companies that make the iPhone 8's physical design look old."

Stylistic Elements

a) Parenthetical Asides: "(in which case, thanks!)," "(Those who are familiar with video games may remember Capcom taking this approach in the'90s when it released like five Street Fighter II variants before jumping to III.)," "(including myself)," etc.

b) Casual/Personal Tone: "Unless you have avoided the internet for the past eight hours and this is the first piece you're reading (in which case, thanks!), you have very likely heard about and seen pictures of Apple's new iPhones." "Some of you may think I'm being superficial, dwelling on the recycled appearance this much." Etc.

c) Rhetorical Questions: "Do you remember the difference between the iPhone 6S and the 6, or the 3GS and the 3G?" "What excuse is there for Apple to not at least trim the iPhone 8's bezels a bit?" "But that's the whole point of being a gadget geek/techie, right?" Etc.

Persuasive Elements

a) Credibility: "Many tech writers (including myself) pointed out that the design was a bit dated and boring." "On the homepages of traditional tech sites like CNET, PC Mag, Wired, a photo and headline about the iPhone X dominates the landing page, while the iPhone 8 is nowhere to be found -- you'd have to scroll down to see coverage." Etc.

b) Passionate Word Choice: "complete lazy rehashes," "dated and boring," "bland," "oh by the way coverage," etc.

c) Counterclaim: "Some of you may think I'm being superficial, dwelling on the recycled appearance this much. But that's the whole point of being a gadget geek/techie, right?" Etc.

Thoroughly read through the entire text given, paying special attention to key points. You will only have time for one full read through. Key points will be quickly exposed through a thesis-like statement and topic sentences. An author's thesis statement most often appears in the introductory paragraph and/or title. Sin's thesis appears in his title, his implied throughout the article, and then is clearly stated at the end.

Sin's Thesis:

Do not buy the I Phone 8 - it's not worth it.

Sin's Topic sentences:

Topic sentences are the first sentence of every paragraph.

"Unless you have avoided the internet for the past eight hours and this is the first piece you're reading (in which case, thanks!), you have very likely heard about and seen pictures of Apple's new iPhones."

"From the second gen I Phone (the 3G) to the I Phone 6S (a period from 2008 to 2016), Apple had followed a two-year cycle for design updates."

"Last year's I Phone 7 broke that trend by keeping the same overall look of the I Phone 6 and 6S."

"Reporters (not columnists, like myself) have to report the I Phone 8's launch straight, but you can almost feel how bored they are with the 8 by the lack of coverage."

Etc.

6

The author's key points will be the structure that your own key points mimic. In this case, Sin's key points are rising a lack of change, a lack of interest because of that change, and the popularity of this feeling. Analyze these points for persuasive techniques, and you have the facts, a personal stylistic technique, and persuasive elements. These three things are the "how" that the sample essay chooses to focus on, but Upton uses other techniques (like those examples given above), as well, to persuade his audience. No two essays will be alike as you and your peers will analyze Upton's work through a personal lens.

Create a clear and concise thesis that states the author's persuasive techniques.

Sample essay's thesis: *He supports his claim by breaking down facts and specs, writing with personal style, and utilizing a range of persuasive elements.*

For detailed analysis, these techniques could reasonably be a list of 2-4 (3, in the sample essay's case). One essay style is to focus each body paragraph on one of those techniques. Another style would be to summarize like techniques in paragraphs together. Paraphrase and quote a few specific lines from the text that support your analysis. Keep any quotes used relatively short. Make sure to always surround a quote with your own words. Introduce the quote, include the quote, and then clearly explain why this quote shows the author's persuasive technique. The essay should be mostly your words, not the authors.

Conclude your essay by pointing out the author's intentions, along with their specific audience. Avoid merely restating your thesis.

Sample essay: *While Apple released two phones, the I Phone X and the I Phone 8, there's only one worth mentioning (the iPhone X) and the other can be forgotten, according to Ben Sin. He works to convince his readers, the consumer and cell phone user, not to buy the I Phone 8. He pulls out all the stops by laying out the facts, getting personal, and utilizing a range of persuasive techniques.*

Answer Sheet

Use a No. 2 pencil. Begin your essay on this page. If you need more space, continue on the next page.

6

_____

_____

_____

_____

_____

_____

_____

_____

_____

_____

_____

_____

_____

_____

_____

_____

_____

_____

_____

_____

_____

_____

_____

_____

_____

_____

6

Sample Essay

The technology of cell phones seems to move forward at breakneck speed, and Apple's products are always at the forefront of that innovation. That is until their recent announcement of the iPhone 8, according to Ben Sin, a tech writer for Forbes. Sin adamantly claims that you should NOT buy the iPhone 8. He supports his claim by breaking down facts and specs, writing with personal style, and utilizing a range of persuasive elements.

Sin knows the past and present of Apple's releases, and he uses these facts to legitimize his claim. Educating the reader, Sin breaks down the pattern of Apple's iPhone releases in the past. Apple has updated its design every two years until 2016, when it broke that cycle. The iPhone 8, then, retains the look of the iPhone 6 for the "fourth straight year". With these facts, Sin shows the reader why they should condemn the new release. Sin continues by explaining the iPhone's "bland" upgrades, highlighting that there are zero changes in hardware. He says, in fact, he has cheap Chinese-made phones that look better than the "laughably large" bezels of the recent iPhone. With these simplified specs, Sim gets his audience to question the lack of change in the iPhone 8, when Apple is clearly capable of so much more. If the Samsung 8 improved upon the Samsung 7, why has Apple let everyone down with the iPhone 8? Sin wants his readers to ask these questions.

Beyond the facts, Sin approaches his reader with a casual and personal style. One way he does this is by speaking to his audience directly in parenthetical comments. One example is right at the beginning of the article where he thanks the reader; "(in which case, thanks!)," and again when he says, "Reporters (not columnists, like myself)". Sin uses these extra comments like whispered secrets in the reader's ear, developing a more trusting relationship. He continues this less professional tone by directly calling out the reader with statements like, "Some of you may think I'm being superficial," and "if you must buy a new Apple phone anytime in the next year, go for the X". Sin's tone aims to make the reader feel like there's a face-to-face, trusting conversation occurring. Lastly, Sin asks rhetorical questions to the reader. Questions like, "Do you remember the difference between the iPhone 6S and the 6, or the 3GS and the 3G?" help the reader realize they've been on the same iPhone journey as Sin and can recognize flaws right along with him.

Sin uses a personal stylistic approach, but he doesn't forget that his article is all about persuasion. He uses passionate word choice to manipulate the reader into feeling his own negative emotions. He refers to the iPhone 8 as a "complete lazy rehash," "dated and boring," "bland," and "not worth it". His willingness to be uncensored, again, works to create a trusting, friendly bond between author and audience. Sin also mentions other tech writers and "traditional tech sites like CNET, PC Mag, Wired" who mimic his feelings in order to boost his credibility. He even quotes an angry twitter user who sums up Sin's sentiments. Sin shows the reader that he's not alone in his disdain for the iPhone 8. Lastly, Sin implements the classic persuasive technique of including a counterclaim. He acknowledges that some may find him superficial, but the phone companies produce more aesthetically pleasing devices all of the time, and the majority fall for it. When Sin anticipates the reader's argument and rebuts it, he deflates any opportunity the reader has to disagree.

While Apple released two phones, the iPhone X and the iPhone 8, there's only one worth mentioning (theiPhone X) and the other can be forgotten, according to Ben Sin. He works to convince his readers, the consumer and cell phone user, not to buy the iPhone 8. He pulls out all the stops by laying out the facts, getting personal, and boosting credibility.

Essay 7

Prompt

As you read the passage below, consider how Flocken uses

- ❏ evidence, such as facts or examples, to support claims.

- ❏ reasoning to develop ideas and to connect claims and evidence.

- ❏ stylistic or persuasive elements, such as word choice or appeals to emotion, to add power to the ideas expressed.

Adapted from Jeff Flocken, "Why Are We Still Hunting Lions?" ©2017 by National Geographic Society. Originally published August 4, 2013.

1. The United States government is considering whether to add lions to the list of species protected by the Endangered Species Act. Such protection would ban the importation of dead trophy lions into the U.S.

2. The proposed move, supported by a coalition of wildlife groups that includes my own, the International Fund for Animal Welfare, raises an obvious question: Why on Earth are we still allowing this animal to be killed for "fun" when it's in danger of disappearing from the wild in our lifetimes?

3. The most recent study, led by a scientist from Duke University, shows that as few as 32,000 lions are left in the wild. Many experts say there could be far fewer.

4. While habitat loss and human-wildlife conflict (often in the form of retaliatory killings after lions kill livestock and sometimes even humans) are the primary causes of the lions' disappearance from Africa's forests and savannahs, trophy hunting adds to the problem. Approximately 600 lions are killed every year on trophy hunts, including lions in populations that are already declining from other threats. These hunts are unsustainable and put more pressure on the species.

5. Unfortunately, Americans are primarily to blame. Approximately 60 percent of all lions killed for sport in Africa are shipped to the U.S. as trophies.

6. There are several reasons why trophy hunting is so bad for lions, beyond the obvious one that it kills healthy members of an imperiled species. The adult male lion is the most sought-after trophy by wealthy foreign hunters. And when an adult male lion is killed, the destabilization of that lion's pride can lead to more lion deaths as outside males compete to take over the pride.

7. Once a new male is in the dominant position, he will often kill the cubs sired by the pride's previous leader, resulting in the loss of an entire lion generation within the pride.

8. Trophy hunting is also counter-evolutionary, as it's based on selectively taking the large, robust, and healthy males from a population for a hunter's trophy room. These are the same crucial individuals that in a natural system would live long, full lives, protecting their mates and cubs and contributing their genes to future generations.

9. Despite the wild claims that trophy hunting brings millions of dollars in revenue to local people in otherwise poor communities, there is no proof of this. Even pro-hunting organizations like the International Council for Game and Wildlife Conservation have reported that only 3 percent of revenue from trophy hunting ever makes it to the communities affected by hunting. The rest goes to national governments or foreign-based outfitters.

10. The money that does come into Africa from hunting pales in comparison to the billions and billions generated from tourists who come just to watch wildlife. If lions and other animals continue to disappear from Africa, this vital source of income - non-consumptive tourism - will end, adversely impacting people all over Africa.

11. Attempts to introduce sustainable methods for sport hunting of lions have been discussed for decades. But the lion population continues to decline, and reform of the hunting industry appears to be far off. Even a new, much-hyped method of targeting aging lions, so that the animals are killed after contributing to the genetic pool, are difficult to pull off and rely on age verification after the lion has already been killed.

12. African lions are the only big cat not currently protected under the Endangered Species Act.

13. Listing African lions as an endangered species and banning trophy imports to the U.S. would send an important message: The African lion is disappearing, and the global community needs to act to stop the trend before it is too late or too costly to reverse.

14. It's a message that won't be heard as long as it is common and legal to kill lions for sport. Why should anyone spend money to protect an animal that a wealthy American can then pay to go kill?

Write an essay in which you explain how Flocken builds an argument to persuade his audience that the U.S. government should make lion hunting illegal. In your essay, analyze how Flocken uses one or more of the features listed above (or features of your own choice) to strengthen the logic and persuasiveness of his argument. Be sure that your analysis focuses on the most relevant features of the passage.

Your essay should not explain whether you agree with Flocken's claims, but rather explain how the author builds an argument to persuade his audience.

Pre-Essay Writing

Read the essay prompt before you read the provided text. Make sure you have a firm grasp on what the prompt is asking you to analyze in your essay. In this case, the prompt specifically says, "explain how Flocken builds an argument to persuade his audience that the U.S. government should make lion hunting illegal". A keyword here is "how". How does Flocken persuade his audience? Recall the bullet points already given to you, asking you to notice evidence such as facts, statistics, or reliable experience, reasoning that connects ideas through logic and explanation, and stylistic or persuasive elements such as word choice, emotional appeal, building credibility, etc. Flocken's techniques will show up in his body paragraphs. As you read, take note of Flocken's use of these things and begin to mentally map out your essay.

Some examples from Flocken's text:

Facts

a) "The United States government is considering whether to add lions to the list of species protected by the Endangered Species Act."

b) "The adult male lion is the most sought-after trophy by wealthy foreign hunters."

c) "Once a new male is in the dominant position, he will often kill the cubs sired by the pride's previous leader, resulting in the loss of an entire lion generation within the pride."

d) "These are the same crucial individuals that in a natural system would live long, full lives, protecting their mates and cubs and contributing their genes to future generations."

Statistics

a) "The most recent study, led by a scientist from Duke University, shows that as few as 32,000 lions are left in the wild. Many experts say there could be far fewer."

b) "Approximately 600 lions are killed every year on trophy hunts, including lions in populations that are already declining from other threats."

c) "Approximately 60 percent of all lions killed for sport in Africa are shipped to the U.S. as trophies."

d) "Even pro-hunting organizations like the International Council for Game and Wildlife Conservation have reported that only 3 percent of revenue from trophy hunting ever makes it to the communities affected by hunting."

Reasoning

a) "Why on Earth are we still allowing this animal to be killed for "fun" when it's in danger of disappearing from the wild in our lifetimes?"

b) "These hunts are unsustainable and put more pressure on the species."

c) "There are several reasons why trophy hunting is so bad for lions, beyond the obvious one that it kills healthy members of an imperiled species."

d) "Listing African lions as an endangered species and banning trophy imports to the U.S. would send an important message: The African lion is disappearing, and the global community needs to act to stop the trend before it is too late or too costly to reverse."

Stylistic Elements

a) Rhetorical questions: "Why should anyone spend money to protect an animal that a wealthy American can then pay to go kill?" "Why on Earth are we still allowing this animal to be killed for "fun" when it's in danger of disappearing from the wild in our lifetimes?"

b) Starting with a conjunction: "And when an adult male lion is killed…" "But the lion population continues to decline…"

c) The colon: "Listing African lions as an endangered species and banning trophy imports to the U.S. would send an important message: The African lion is disappearing, and the global community needs to act to stop the trend before it is too late or too costly to reverse." Etc.

Persuasive Elements

a) Emotional appeal: "Once a new male is in the dominant position, he will often kill the cubs sired by the pride's previous leader, resulting in the loss of an entire lion generation within the pride." Etc.

b) Counterclaim: "Despite the wild claims that trophy hunting brings millions of dollars in revenue to local people in otherwise poor communities, there is no proof of this." Etc.

c) Credibility: "Even pro-hunting organizations like the International Council for Game and Wildlife Conservation have reported that only 3 percent of revenue from trophy hunting ever makes it to the communities affected by hunting." Etc.

Thoroughly read through the entire text given, paying special attention to key points. You will only have time for one full read through. Key points will be quickly exposed through a thesis-like statement and topic sentences. An author's thesis statement most often appears in the introductory paragraph and sometimes title. Flocken's thesis is implied throughout the paper and becomes especially clear at the end.

Flocken's Thesis:

Listing African lions as an endangered species and banning trophy imports to the U.S. would send an important message: The African lion is disappearing, and the global community needs to act to stop the trend before it is too late or too costly to reverse.

Flocken's Topic sentences:

Topic sentences are the first sentence of every paragraph.

"The United States government is considering whether to add lions to the list of species protected by the Endangered Species Act."

"The most recent study, led by a scientist from Duke University, shows that as few as 32,000 lions are left in the wild."

"Unfortunately, Americans are primarily to blame."

"There are several reasons why trophy hunting is so bad for lions, beyond the obvious one that it kills healthy members of an imperiled species."

Etc.

The author's key points will be the structure that your own key points mimic. In this case, Flocken's key points are decreasing numbers, affected lion environments, and money distribution. Analyze these points for persuasive techniques, and you have statistics, facts, and counterclaim. These three things are the "how" that the sample essay chooses to focus on, but Flocken uses other techniques (like those examples given above), as well, to persuade his audience. No two essays will be alike as you and your peers will analyze Flocken's work through a personal lens.

Create a clear and concise thesis that states the author's persuasive techniques.

Sample essay's thesis: *He supports his claim by using statistics, citing facts, and addressing counterclaims.*

For detailed analysis, these techniques could reasonably be a list of 2-4 (3, in the sample essay's case). One essay style is to focus each body paragraph on one of those techniques. Another style would be to summarize like techniques in paragraphs together. Paraphrase and quote a few specific lines from the text that support your analysis. Keep any quotes used relatively short. Make sure to always surround a quote with your own words. Introduce the quote, include the quote, and then clearly explain why this quote shows the author's persuasive technique. The essay should be mostly your words, not the authors.

Conclude your essay by pointing out the author's intentions, along with their specific audience. Avoid merely restating your thesis.

Sample essay: *The U.S. government, according to Flocken, has no real reason for stalling efforts to put the African lion on the endangered species list and making trophy hunting illegal. Flocken has science, evolution, and logic on his side. He wants a ban on lion trophy hunting, and he wants it now.*

Answer Sheet

Use a No. 2 pencil. Begin your essay on this page. If you need more space, continue on the next page.

7

_____

_____

_____

_____

_____

_____

_____

_____

_____

_____

_____

_____

_____

_____

_____

_____

_____

_____

_____

_____

7

7

Sample Essay

For some in the United States, exotic game, like hunting lions, is an adventure worth buying. For others, like Jeff Flocken, lion hunting is sport worth banning. Jeff Flocken, in his article for National Geographic, argues that the United States government needs to make lion hunting illegal. He supports his claim by using statistics, citing facts, and addressing counterclaims.

Flocken makes it clear to his audience that science and statistics are on his side. His first statistic aims to be most shocking, that "only 32,000 lions are left in the wild". Flocken shares this surprising number to the reader, portraying that lions are, indeed, in danger of going extinct. He continues to show the impact humans have on lions by sharing that around 600 lions are taken home each year as trophies, and sadly, 60 percent of those trophies are shipped to the U.S. Flocken points out these numbers in an effort to show the U.S. government that lion hunting is our nation's problem. For readers who may think that lion hunting boosts the economy of surrounding communities, statistics show only 3 percent make it back to them. Flocken's choice of statistic here, aims to show that there is no real benefit to American's killing off lions, no benefit beyond detrimental entertainment.

Similarly, Flocken turns to facts to explain the impact of lion hunting. He explains that hunting not only affects the lion killed, it effects the pride, as well. Most lions sought after in a hunt are male adults, and when a male adult dies, other male lions kill each other off in a fight for power. The winner will kill the sons of the previous pride leader. Flocken includes this fact to show his reader that lion hunting messes with the natural order of things. When a hunter kills one lion, he may actually be killing many. To further this concept, Flocken explains, "Trophy hunting is also counter-evolutionary, as it's based on selectively taking the large, robust, and healthy males from a population for a hunter's trophy room." If Americans are killing off the protector, future generations are in danger. Despite all of this, Flocken points out that lions are the only big cats not protected under the endangered species list. Juxtaposing this last fact with the proof that lions are suffering large losses shows the reader an obvious area of solution.

To convert any doubters, Flocken addresses several specific objections people may have in a counterclaim. Again, some may argue that lion hunting is positive to the economy of African communities. Flocken has anticipated this argument and dismisses it by explaining that even "pro-hunting organizations like the International Council for Game and Wildlife Conservation" know this is untrue. Not only that, but surrounding communities make a lot more money from tourists who merely watch the lions. Flocken shows the reader that the money argument is invalid, especially since all money will be gone if lions go extinct. He even addresses those who believe lion hunting can still exist with the introduction of sustainable methods. Flocken reinforces his sentiments that sustainable methods don't matter; lion numbers continue dropping off.

The U.S. government, according to Flocken, has no real reason for stalling efforts to put the African lion on the endangered species list and making trophy hunting illegal. Flocken has science, evolution, and logic on his side. He wants a ban on lion trophy hunting, and he wants it now.

Essay 8

Prompt

As you read the passage below, consider how Upton uses

- ❏ evidence, such as facts or examples, to support claims.

- ❏ reasoning to develop ideas and to connect claims and evidence.

- ❏ stylistic or persuasive elements, such as word choice or appeals to emotion, to add power to the ideas expressed.

Adapted from Buzz Aldrin, "Forget the Moon. Let's Go to Mars." ©2017 by National Geographic. Originally published May 12, 2013.

1. As an Apollo 11 astronaut, I stood on the talcum-like lunar dust just a few feet from the Eagle, the lander that carried Neil Armstrong and me to the bleak, crater-pocked moon. Looking around at my surroundings on that July day in 1969, I called it "magnificent desolation."

2. Whenever I gaze up at the moon, I feel like I'm on a time machine. I am back to that precious pinpoint of time, standing on the foreboding - yet beautiful - Sea of Tranquility. I could see our shining blue planet Earth poised in the darkness of space.

3. Virtually the entire world took that extraordinary journey along with the crew of Apollo 11. We were supported by hundreds of thousands of American workers, the greatest can-do team ever assembled on the face of the Earth. That team was comprised of scientists and engineers, metallurgists and meteorologists, flight directors, navigators, and suit testers - as well as policy makers. So many devoted their lives and professional energies, minds, and hearts to our mission and to the following Apollo expeditions. Those Americans embraced commitment and quality to surmount the unknowns with us.

4. Fast forward to nearly 45 years later. Today, I see the moon in a different light.

5. America won the "moon race" more than four decades ago. We do not need to engage in that contest again. Instead, we should set our sights on a permanent human presence on Mars. There is no compelling reason that this can't be done, but great care must be taken that precious government dollars necessary for the great leap to Mars are not sidetracked to the moon.

6. Robotic exploration of the Red Planet - including the highly capable NASA Mars rover Curiosity - provides us a window on a world that can be a true home-away-from-home for future adventurers. Mars has been flown by, orbited, smacked into, radar inspected, and rocketed onto, as well as bounced upon, rolled over, shoveled, drilled into, baked, and even laser blasted.

7. Still to come - being stepped on.

8. The first footfalls on Mars will mark a momentous milestone, an enterprise that requires human tenacity matched with technology to anchor ourselves on another world. Exploring Mars is a far different venture than Apollo expeditions to the moon; it necessitates leaving our home planet on lengthy missions with a constrained return capability. Once humans are at distant Mars, there is a very narrow window during which they can return to Earth - a fundamental distinction between our reaching the moon and sailing outward to Mars. Therefore, we need to start thinking about building permanence on the Red Planet and what it takes to do that. It is a vision of the extension of humanity to Mars.

9. As outlined in my book Mission to Mars: My Vision for Space Exploration, we can implement a step-by-step vision to plunge deeper and deeper outward. Part of the plan is a sequential buildup of a spaceship network that coincides with an ever-increasing escalation of action on the moon and Mars. The Earth, the moon, and Mars become busy places as people, cargo, and commerce navigate through the inner solar system. (See video: Buzz Aldrin discusses new book on possible Mars mission)

10. When Neil and I stepped upon the surface of the moon at Tranquility Base, we fulfilled a dream held by humankind for centuries. As inscribed on the plaque affixed to the ladder of our lander: "We Came in Peace for All Mankind." It was, truly, one small step. But more steps are needed.

11. Nowadays, my dedication - indeed, my passion - is focused on forging America's future in space, guided by two principles: a continuously expanding human presence in space, and global leadership in space.

8

12. To move forward, what's required is a unified space agenda based on exploration, science, development, commerce, and security. For instance, our work on the moon should be limited to robots assigned to scientific, commercial, and other private-sector work. We need a unified international effort to explore and utilize the moon. It would be a partnership that involves commercial enterprise and other nations building upon the Apollo legacy.

13. Earth isn't the only world for us anymore.

14. There's an opportunity to make a bold, Kennedy-esque statement in July 2019, on the occasion of the 50th anniversary of the first humans to land on the moon: "I believe this nation should commit itself, within two decades, to commencing American permanence on the planet Mars."

15. In reaching outward with method and intent to Mars, and helping others go where we have already gone, America is once again in the business of a momentous and future-focused space exploration program.

16. Let's get rolling . . . and roll up our sleeves and begin.

Write an essay in which you explain how Aldrin builds an argument to persuade his audience that space exploration should focus on making permanent human presence on Mars. In your essay, analyze how Aldrin uses one or more of the features listed above (or features of your own choice) to strengthen the logic and persuasiveness of his argument. Be sure that your analysis focuses on the most relevant features of the passage.

Your essay should not explain whether you agree with Aldrin's claims, but rather explain how the author builds an argument to persuade his audience.

Pre-Essay Writing

Read the essay prompt before you read the provided text. Make sure you have a firm grasp on what the prompt is asking you to analyze in your essay. In this case, the prompt specifically says, "explain how Aldrin builds an argument to persuade his audience that space exploration should focus on making permanent human presence on Mars". A keyword here is "how". How does Aldrin persuade his audience? Recall the bullet points already given to you, asking you to notice evidence such as facts, statistics, or reliable experience, reasoning that connects ideas through logic and explanation, and stylistic or persuasive elements such as word choice, emotional appeal, building credibility, etc. Aldrin's techniques will show up in his body paragraphs. As you read, take note of Aldrin's use of these things and begin to mentally map out your essay.

Some examples from Aldrin's text:

Facts

a) "Looking around at my surroundings on that July day in 1969, I called it 'magnificent desolation.'"

b) "That team was comprised of scientists and engineers, metallurgists and meteorologists, flight directors, navigators, and suit testers - as well as policy makers."

c) "America won the "moon race" more than four decades ago."

d) "Mars is a far different venture than Apollo expeditions to the moon; it necessitates leaving our home planet on lengthy missions with a constrained return capability."

Reasoning

a) "Robotic exploration of the Red Planet - including the highly capable NASA Mars rover Curiosity—provides us a window on a world that can be a true home-away-from-home for future adventurers."

b) "Once humans are at distant Mars, there is a very narrow window during which they can return to Earth

- a fundamental distinction between our reaching the moon and sailing outward to Mars. Therefore, we need to start thinking about building permanence on the Red Planet and what it takes to do that."

c) "To move forward, what's required is a unified space agenda based on exploration, science, development, commerce, and security. For instance, our work on the moon should be limited to robots assigned to scientific, commercial, and other private-sector work."

d) "In reaching outward with method and intent to Mars, and helping others go where we have already gone, America is once again in the business of a momentous and future-focused space exploration program."

Stylistic Elements

a) **Alliteration:** "The first footfalls on Mars will mark a momentous milestone," "focused on forging America's future," etc.

b) **Flattering word choice:** "precious," "highly capable," "vision of extension," "dream," etc.

c) **Reversal:** "We do not need to engage in that contest again."

d) **Prepositional words and phrases:** Whenever I gaze up at the moon," "Today," "Once humans are at distant Mars," etc.

Persuasive Elements

a) **Wordplay:** "Still to come - being stepped on," etc.

b) **Emotional appeal:** "When Neil and I stepped upon the surface of the moon at Tranquility Base, we fulfilled a dream held by humankind for centuries," etc.

c) **Credibility:** "That team was comprised of scientists and engineers, metallurgists and meteorologists, flight directors, navigators, and suit testers - as well as policy makers," etc.

Thoroughly read through the entire text given, paying special attention to key points. You will only have time for one full read through. Key points will be quickly exposed through a thesis-like statement and topic sentences. An author's thesis statement most often appears in the introductory paragraph and title. Aldrin's can be seen in the title and after brief background about his experience with the lunar landing.

Aldrin's Thesis:

We do not need to engage in that contest again. Instead, we should set our sights on a permanent human presence on Mars.

Aldrin's Topic sentences:

Topic sentences are the first sentence of every paragraph.

"As an Apollo 11 astronaut, I stood on the talcum-like lunar dust just a few feet from the Eagle, the lander that carried Neil Armstrong and me to the bleak, crater-pocked moon."

"Virtually the entire world took that extraordinary journey along with the crew of Apollo 11."

"America won the "moon race" more than four decades ago."

"Robotic exploration of the Red Planet - including the highly capable NASA Mars rover Curiosity - provides us a window on a world that can be a true home-away-from-home for future adventurers."

Etc.

The author's key points will be the structure that your own key points mimic. In this case, Aldrin's key points are rising an old history of landing on the moon, change for the future, and a need for support in someone trustworthy. Analyze these points for persuasive techniques, and you have facts, stylistic techniques, and persuasive elements. These three things are the "how" that the sample essay chooses to focus on, but Aldrin uses other techniques (like those examples given above), as well, to persuade his audience. No two essays will be alike as you and your peers will analyze Aldrin's work through a personal lens.

Create a clear and concise thesis that states the author's persuasive techniques.

Sample essay's thesis: *He supports his claim by using clear facts, purposeful stylistic techniques, and clever persuasive elements.*

For detailed analysis, these techniques could reasonably be a list of 2-4 (3, in the sample essay's case). One essay style is to focus each body paragraph on one of those techniques. Another style would be to summarize like techniques in paragraphs together. Paraphrase and quote a few specific lines from the text that support your analysis. Keep any quotes used relatively short. Make sure to always surround a quote with your own words. Introduce the quote, include the quote, and then clearly explain why this quote shows the author's persuasive technique. The essay should be mostly your words, not the authors.

Conclude your essay by pointing out the author's intentions, along with their specific audience. Avoid merely restating your thesis.

Sample essay: *According to Buzz Aldrin, landing on the moon was a precious experience, but it's time to seek out a new and improved moment like that one. He works to bring American readers, especially those in influential government positions, over to his side by breaking down the facts of the past and present, implementing purposeful stylistic techniques, and using wordplay and credibility. Aldrin hasn't been on Mars, but his passion for the subject is as clear as the memory of his 1969 lunar landing.*

Answer Sheet

Use a No. 2 pencil. Begin your essay on this page. If you need more space, continue on the next page.

8

8

Sample Essay

Since space exploration began in America, its focus has been the moon. Neil Armstrong and Buzz Aldrin actually landed on the moon in 1969, and decades later, it remains the only place man has stepped foot on outside of the Earth. Buzz Aldrin claims that it's time to leave the moon behind and put all American space exploration efforts into making permanent human presence on Mars. He supports his claim by using clear facts, purposeful stylistic techniques, and clever persuasive elements.

Buzz Aldrin has worked first-hand on efforts to grow American knowledge of the moon and Mars, so he has the simple facts. His recollection of American homes tuning-in for the moon landing, and the involvement of "scientists and engineers, metallurgists and meteorologists, flight directors, navigators, and suit testers - as well as policy makers" shows the modern reader the novelty that existed around the event 44 years ago. Aldrin nonchalantly brings up this fact, along with its attached date, to demonstrate how long ago the lunar landing was and how stagnant we've been in comparison. He even does the math: 4 decades. Aldrin also knows the facts going forward. He clearly spells out the complications of aiming to land on Mars, expeditions with "constrained return capability" where astronauts have tiny windows of time to get back to Earth. Aldrin brings up this fact not to discourage readers but to show the importance and urgency of finding permanence on Mars.

Aldrin uses more than facts to prove his point; he thinks of the American reader and chooses his words wisely throughout the article. Giving a feeling of moving forward, Aldrin utilizes prepositional words and phrases. They transition from, "As an Apollo 11 astronaut," to, "Nowadays," to "In reaching outward with method and intent to Mars". Aldrin aims to take you into the future with him. Aldrin also uses word choice that works to paint Mars exploration in a positive light. He attaches the idea of human presence on Mars to words like, "vision," "home-away-from-home," "dream," "momentous and future-focused". He purposefully chooses these words to associate flattery with his claim.

Lastly, Aldrin gets clever with his persuasive elements, using snarky wordplay and boasting of his credibility. Twice, Aldrin makes a clear point through wordplay, almost like the punch line to a joke. After running through the long list of research achieved on Mars ("flown by, orbited, smacked into, radar inspected...etc.), he states the only thing that hasn't happened: stepped on. This abrupt statement aims to have the reader question why we haven't gone there yet. It's the next step. At the end of his article, Aldrin uses this tongue-and-cheek wordplay again when he states, "Let's get rolling . . . and roll up our sleeves and begin." These punch line deliveries are an appeal to the reader for action. The reader should listen because, as he notes, Aldrin has credibility on his side. Not only was he an astronaut working directly with a long list of scientists and professionals, but he continues to be involved in space exploration. He has even written a book about Mars and this very subject, Mission to Mars: My Vision for Space Exploration. With all of these credentials, Aldrin shows off his trustworthiness.

According to Buzz Aldrin, landing on the moon was a precious experience, but it's time to seek out a new and improved moment like that one. He works to bring American readers, especially those in influential government positions, over to his side by breaking down the facts of the past and present, implementing purposeful stylistic techniques, and using wordplay and credibility. Aldrin hasn't been on Mars, but his passion for the subject is as clear as the memory of his 1969 lunar landing.

Essay 9

Prompt

As you read the passage below, consider how Reilly uses

❑ evidence, such as facts or examples, to support claims.

❑ reasoning to develop ideas and to connect claims and evidence.

❑ stylistic or persuasive elements, such as word choice or appeals to emotion, to add power to the ideas expressed.

Adapted From Rick Reilly, "Nothing But Nets" ©2015 by Sports Illustrated. Originally published May 01, 2006.

1. I've never asked for anything before, right? Well, sorry, I'm asking now.

2. We need nets.

3. Not hoop nets, soccer nets or lacrosse nets. Not New Jersey Nets or dot-nets or clarinets. Mosquito nets.

4. See, nearly 3,000 kids die every day in Africa from malaria. And according to the World Health Organization, transmission of the disease would be reduced by 60% with the use of mosquito nets and prompt treatment for the infected.

5. Three thousand kids! That's a 9/11 every day!

6. Put it this way: Let's say your little Justin's Kickin' Kangaroos have a big youth soccer tournament on Saturday. There are 15 kids on the team, 10 teams in the tourney. And there are 20 of these tournaments going on all over town. Suddenly, every one of these kids gets chills and fever, then starts throwing up and then gets short of breath. And in seven to 10 days, they're all dead of malaria.

7. We got a get these nets. They're coated with an insecticide and cost between $4 and $6. You need about $10, all told, to get them shipped and installed. Some nets can cover a family of four. And they last four years. If we can cut the spread of disease, 10 bucks means a kid might get to live. Make it $20 and more kids are saved.

8. So, here's the ask: If you have ever gotten a thrill by throwing, kicking, knocking, dunking, slamming, putting up, cutting down or jumping over a net, please go to a special site we've set up through the United Nations. The address is: UNFoundation.org/malaria. Then just look for the big SI's Nothing But Net logo (or call 202-887-9040) and donate $20. Bang. You might have just saved a kid's life.

9. Or would you rather have the new Beastie Boys CD?

10. You're a coach, parent, player, gym teacher or even just a fan who likes watching balls fly into nets, send $20. You saved a life. Take the rest of the day off.

11. You have ever had a net in the driveway, front lawn or on your head at McDonald's, send $20. You ever imagined Angelina Jolie in fishnets, $20. So, you stay home and eat on the dinette. You'll live.

12. Hey, Dick's Sporting Goods. You have 255 stores. How about you kick in a dime every time you sell a net? Hey, NBA players, hockey stars and tennis pros, how about you donate $20 every time one of your shots hits the net? Maria Sharapova, you don't think this applies to you just because you're Russian? Nyet!

13. I tried to think how many times I have said or written the word "net" in 28 years of sports writing, and I came up with, conservatively, 20,000. So, I've already started us off with a $20,000 donation. That's a whole lot of lives. Together, we could come up with $1 million, net. How many lives would that save? More than 50 times the population of Nett Lake, Minn.

14. I know what you're thinking: Yeah, but bottom line, how much of our $1 million goes to nets? All of it. Thanks to Ted Turner, who donated $1 billion to create the U.N. Foundation, which covers all the overhead, "every cent will go to nets," says Andrea Gay, the U.N. Foundation's Director of Children's Health.

15. Nets work! Bill and Melinda Gates have just about finished single-handedly covering every bed in Zambia. Maybe we can't cover an entire Zambia, but I bet we could put a serious dent in Malawi.

16. It's not like we're betting on some scientist somewhere coming up with a cure. And it's not like warlords are going to hijack a truckload of nets. "Theoretically, if every person in Africa slept at night under a net," says Gay, "nobody need ever die of malaria again." You talk about a net profit.

17. My God, think of all the nets that are taken for granted in sports! Ping-Pong nets. Batting cage nets. Terrell Owens's bassinet. If you sit behind the plate at a baseball game, you watch the action through a net. You download the highlights on Netscape and forward it on the net to your friend Ben-net while eating Raisi-nets. Sports is nothing but net. So next time you think of a net, go to that website and click yourself happy. Way more fun than your fantasy bowling league, dude.

18. One last vignette: A few years back, we took the family to Tanzania, which is ravaged by malaria now. We visited a school and played soccer with the kids. Must've been 50 on each team, running and laughing. A taped-up wad of newspapers was the ball and two rocks were the goal. Most fun I ever had getting whipped. When we got home, we sent some balls and nets.

19. I kick myself now for that. How many of those kids are dead because we sent the wrong nets?

Write an essay in which you explain how Reilly builds an argument to persuade his audience that their money is best well spent buying mosquito nets for Africa. In your essay, analyze how Reilly uses one or more of the features listed above (or features of your own choice) to strengthen the logic and persuasiveness of his argument. Be sure that your analysis focuses on the most relevant features of the passage.

Your essay should not explain whether you agree with Reilly's claims, but rather explain how the author builds an argument to persuade his audience.

Pre-Essay Writing

Read the essay prompt before you read the provided text. Make sure you have a firm grasp on what the prompt is asking you to analyze in your essay. In this case, the prompt specifically says, "explain how Reilly builds an argument to persuade his audience that their money is best well spent buying mosquito nets for Africa". A keyword here is "how". How does Reilly persuade his audience? Recall the bullet points already given to you, asking you to notice evidence such as facts, statistics, or reliable experience, reasoning that connects ideas through logic and explanation, and stylistic or persuasive elements such as word choice, emotional appeal, building credibility, etc. Reilly's techniques will show up in his body paragraphs. As you read, take note of Reilly's use of these things and begin to mentally map out your essay.

9

Some examples from Reilly's text:

Facts

a) "They're coated with an insecticide and cost between $4 and $6. You need about $10, all told, to get them shipped and installed."

b) "The address is: UNFoundation.org/malaria. Then just look for the big SI's Nothing But Net logo (or call 202-887-9040) and donate $20."

c) "Thanks to Ted Turner, who donated $1 billion to create the U.N. Foundation, which covers all the overhead, "every cent will go to nets," says Andrea Gay, the U.N. Foundation's Director of Children's Health."

d) "Bill and Melinda Gates have just about finished single-handedly covering every bed in Zambia."

Statistics

a) "See, nearly 3,000 kids die every day in Africa from malaria."

b) "And according to the World Health Organization, transmission of the disease would be reduced by 60% with the use of mosquito nets and prompt treatment for the infected."

c) "I tried to think how many times I have said or written the word "net" in 28 years of sports writing, and I came up with, conservatively, 20,000."

d) "How many lives would that save? More than 50 times the population of Nett Lake, Minn."

Reasoning

a) "That's a 9/11 every day!"

b) "If we can cut the spread of disease, 10 bucks means a kid might get to live. Make it $20 and more kids are saved."

c) "So, you stay home and eat on the dinette. You'll live."

d) "It's not like we're betting on some scientist somewhere coming up with a cure. And it's not like warlords are going to hijack a truckload of nets. "Theoretically, if every person in Africa slept at night under a net," says Gay, "nobody need ever die of malaria again.""

Stylistic Elements

a) **Wordplay:** "net profit," "Netscape," "Raisinets," "clarinets," etc.

b) **Fragments:** "Not hoop nets, soccer nets or lacrosse nets. Not New Jersey Nets or dot-nets or clarinets. Mosquito nets." "Or would you rather have the new Beastie Boys CD?" Etc.

c) **Casual/Personal tone:** "I've never asked for anything before, right? Well, sorry, I'm asking now." "We got a get these nets." "You're a coach, parent, player, gym teacher or even just a fan who likes watching balls fly into nets, send $20. You saved a life. Take the rest of the day off." Etc.

Persuasive Elements

a) **Emotional appeal:** "Most fun I ever had getting whipped. When we got home, we sent some balls and nets. I kick myself now for that. How many of those kids are dead because we sent the wrong nets?"

b) **Credibility:** "Bill and Melinda Gates have just about finished single-handedly covering every bed in Zambia. Maybe we can't cover an entire Zambia, but I bet we could put a serious dent in Malawi."

c) **Personal examples:** "Let's say your little Justin's Kickin' Kangaroos have a big youth soccer tournament on Saturday. There are 15 kids on the team, 10 teams in the tourney. And there are 20 of these tournaments going on all over town. Suddenly, every one of these kids gets chills and fever, then starts throwing up and then gets short of breath. And in seven to 10 days, they're all dead of malaria."

Thoroughly read through the entire text given, paying special attention to key points. You will only have time for one full read through. Key points will be quickly exposed through a thesis-like statement and topic sentences. An author's thesis statement most often appears in the introductory paragraph. While smaller variations of Reilly's thesis show up at the beginning of his article, the real pitch comes in a bit further, after he gives some background.

Reilly's Thesis:

If you have ever gotten a thrill by throwing, kicking, knocking, dunking, slamming, putting up, cutting down or jumping over a net, please go to a special site we've set up through the United Nations. The address is: UNFoundation.org/malaria. Then just look for the big SI's Nothing But Net logo (or call 202-887-9040) and donate $20.

Reilly's Topic sentences:

Topic sentences are the first sentence of every paragraph.

"We need nets."

"See, nearly 3,000 kids die every day in Africa from malaria."

"You're a coach, parent, player, gym teacher or even just a fan who likes watching balls fly into nets, send $20."

"I know what you're thinking: Yeah, but bottom line, how much of our $1 million goes to nets?"

Etc.

The author's key points will be the structure that your own key points mimic. In this case, Reilly's key points are malaria death tolls, opportunity to give, and relevance of the problem. Analyze these points for persuasive techniques, and you have facts and statistics, personal tone, and wordplay. These three things are the "how" that the sample essay chooses to focus on, but Reilly uses other techniques (like those examples given above), as well, to persuade his audience. No two essays will be alike as you and your peers will analyze Reilly's work through a personal lens.

Create a clear and concise thesis that states the author's persuasive techniques.

Sample essay's thesis: *He supports his argument by using facts and statistics, by using a personal tone, and by using wordplay.*

For detailed analysis, these techniques could reasonably be a list of 2-4 (3, in the sample essay's case). One essay style is to focus each body paragraph on one of those techniques. Another style would be to summarize like techniques in paragraphs together. Paraphrase and quote a few specific lines from the text that support your analysis. Keep any quotes used relatively short. Make sure to always surround a quote with your own words. Introduce the quote, include the quote, and then clearly explain why this quote shows the author's persuasive technique. The essay should be mostly your words, not the authors.

Conclude your essay by pointing out the author's intentions, along with their specific audience. Avoid merely restating your thesis.

Sample essay: *Nets are an important ingredient of sports life, but in Africa, nets are an important ingredient to life, in general. Reilly practically begs his readers to learn from his own experience and new knowledge, to buy mosquito nets, and to save a life. His professionalism drops, and he pulls out all the stops in order to get sports enthusiast to spare $10 and save kids from the pain of malaria.*

Answer Sheet

Use a No. 2 pencil. Begin your essay on this page. If you need more space, continue on the next page.

_____

_____

_____

_____

_____

_____

_____

_____

9

_____

_____

_____

_____

_____

_____

_____

_____

_____

_____

9

9

Sample Essay

Sports Illustrated is normally a magazine that focuses on all things sports. In Rick Reilly's article, "Nothing But Nets," though, he addresses his athletic readership, persuading them to spend their money on mosquito nets for Africa, instead of sports. He supports his argument by using facts and statistics, by using a personal tone, and by using wordplay.

Early on, Reilly uses facts and statistics to show the impact a single mosquito net could have on African kids. Mosquitoes spread malaria, and in Africa, that means "nearly 3,000 kids die every day". For Reilly's audience, an audience of first world country citizens, malaria isn't even on small list of worries, so this is a shocking statistic. He continues to say that a simple mosquito net would stop the spread of malaria by 60%. Again, a statistic so large for a solution so simple is a shocking realization for Reilly to bring to his audience. If one mosquito could save lives, how easy would it be for his audience to provide a life-saving net? Reilly quickly provides the math to this question; a net sold and shipped is a clean-cut $10. More money equals more nets and more lives. Reilly supplies the easy facts on how to buy these nets online. The straightforward and simple math approach that Reilly takes to the facts of Africa's malaria issue aims to make it hard for his audience to excuse themselves from taking action. He relays the U.N. Foundation's Director of Children's Health, Andrea Gay's, message in saying that if everyone in Africa were to sleep under a net, nobody would die of malaria. That's a difficult fact for Reilly's readers to ignore.

Reilly isn't all math, though; he takes a personal approach to the malaria issue, addressing his audience casually, and coming up with relatable scenarios. He starts by apologizing to his audience, stating that he never asks for anything, but he's doing so now. Reilly talks to his readers as if they are long-time friends. This approach establishes sense of honesty and credibility. He continues this more casual approach throughout the entire article, using pronouns like "I" and "you" and "we". It's as if he is having a conversation with his readers, further establishing a relationship. In this conversation, he adds real-life scenarios, like when he asks them to imagine their own child's soccer team, league, and 20 other tournaments around town all dying at the same time. That's what malaria does. This personal example hits closer to home for Reilly's audience. He takes it even more personal at the end of his essay when he realizes he missed out on his own opportunity to save lives. After playing soccer with kids in Tanzania, he sent them soccer balls and nets only to realize, "How many of those kids are dead because we sent the wrong nets?" He seems to say, "Don't be like me".

Another powerful tool that Reilly employs for his persuasion is wordplay. To a Sports Illustrated audience, a net seems to have a specific connotation, but Reilly shows that the issue with malaria allows them to think about nets in a different way. He urges the reader to donate nets if they've ever had a net in their driveway, in their lawn, on their head, or even if they've imagined fishnets on Angelina Jolie. The mosquito nets are a more important purchase. Not only does Reilly use a bit of humor with his wordplay here, but he also shows the prevalence of a net in the first world country. He points out this prevalence directly when he realizes he's probably said the word "net" around 20,000 times in his sports writing career. Never once has he thought about it in terms of saving a life, until now. He points out this word associated realization, so that the audience's mindset will change too, and then he blasts them with the word. "My God, think of all the nets that are taken for granted in sports!" Reilly lists different sport nets, Netscape, internet, your friend Ben-net, Raisinets, vignettes, etc. It's like he doesn't want the audience to hear the word "net" without thinking about Africa's need.

Nets are an important ingredient of sports life, but in Africa, nets are an important ingredient to life, in general. Reilly practically begs his readers to learn from his own experience and new knowledge, to buy mosquito nets, and to save a life. His professionalism drops, and he pulls out all the stops in order to get sports enthusiast to spare $10 and save kids from the pain of malaria.

9

Essay 10

Prompt

As you read the passage below, consider how Lemmon uses

- ❏ evidence, such as facts or examples, to support claims.

- ❏ reasoning to develop ideas and to connect claims and evidence.

- ❏ stylistic or persuasive elements, such as word choice or appeals to emotion, to add power to the ideas expressed.

Adapted from Kindy Lemmon, "Chronic pain sufferers need access to opioids" ©2017 by Deseret News. Originally published September 14, 2017.

1. My 26-year-old daughter, Madison, is an extremely intelligent, articulate, creative and beautiful young woman. Anyone blessed with these attributes should be well on their way to a wonderful and fulfilling life. But Madison is suffering in ways that most people could never imagine. Diagnosed at 13 years old with Complex Regional Pain Syndrome, formerly known as Reflex Sympathetic Dystrophy (CRPS/RSD), an incurable and progressive chronic pain disease of the sympathetic nervous system, she lives every day in severe pain.

2. CRPS/RSD is ranked as the most painful form of chronic pain that exists today by the McGill Pain Index. With the advice of numerous physicians over the last 13 years, we have tried every possible remedy and every possible treatment. None of them worked. So many days, I can only hold her in my arms as she cries in agony. The only thing that eases her suffering slightly is her prescription of opioid medication. Yet the government, in a short-sighted effort to combat widespread opioid abuse, wants to take Madison's lifeline away. She, along with many others in her situation, are apparently considered collateral damage.

3. Collateral damage is not acceptable. Our military does the best it can to minimize collateral damage on the innocent and unintended targets even if it means sparing the intended targets. This is supported by not only by our government, but by the international community as well. And it should be that way. It's compassionate.

4. Why, then, is our government inflicting cruel and unusual punishment for innocent victims here at home? They are putting extreme pressure upon physicians, under the threat of being removed from their practice, to reduce and/or eliminate the levels of prescribed opioids to all patients. But there will be collateral damage to this. Tens of thousands of people who have chronic pain will suffer. For them, there is no relief without opioid medication, and for whom the reduction or the elimination of their medication will cause unspeakable pain and even death.

5. The United Nations Universal Declaration of Human Rights states in Article 5, "No one shall be subjected to torture or to cruel, inhuman or degrading treatment or punishment." Medical doctors in the United States take the Hippocratic Oath that states, "I will follow that system of regimen which, according to my ability and judgment, I consider for the benefit of my patients, and abstain from whatever is deleterious and mischievous."

6. How can we be in direct conflict to both the Declaration of Human Rights and the Hippocratic Oath, and cause immense suffering to those of us who are in chronic, incurable pain? How can we reconcile the fact that, as a country, we can show compassion and lend assistance to refugees, and send food and medical aid to Third World countries, yet allow our family and friends to be denied the medication they need to survive?

7. It is because we are only being shown one side of this story. What we are not shown are the millions of patients in the USA alone who, but for their opioid medication, would be left in constant and excruciating pain. Taking away their right to be treated for their pain is the real opioid crisis.

8. Sadly, there are thousands of people who die from the over-the-counter drug ibuprofen every year. There are tens of thousands of people dying from their antidepressants and benzodiazepines. There are hundreds of thousands of people who die from complications associated with anticoagulants. Although these numbers are tragic, we would not want to see the physicians associated with these prescriptions threatened. This, however, is exactly what is happening in the case of the opioid crisis.

9. This is not acceptable.

Write an essay in which you explain how Lemmon builds an argument to persuade her audience that taking away opioids for chronic pain sufferers is the real opioid crisis. In your essay, analyze how Lemmon uses one or more of the features listed above (or features of your own choice) to strengthen the logic and persuasiveness of his argument. Be sure that your analysis focuses on the most relevant features of the passage.

Your essay should not explain whether you agree with Lemmon's claims, but rather explain how the author builds an argument to persuade her audience.

 **Pre-Essay Writing**

Read the essay prompt before you read the provided text. Make sure you have a firm grasp on what the prompt is asking you to analyze in your essay. In this case, the prompt specifically says, "explain how Lemmon builds an argument to persuade her audience that taking away opioids for chronic pain sufferers is the real opioid crisis". A keyword here is "how". How does Lemmon persuade her audience? Recall the bullet points already given to you, asking you to notice evidence such as facts, statistics, or reliable experience, reasoning that connects ideas through logic and explanation, and stylistic or persuasive elements such as word choice, emotional appeal, building credibility, etc. Lemmon's techniques will show up in her body paragraphs. As you read, take note of Lemmon's use of these things and begin to mentally map out your essay.

Some examples from Lemmon's text:

Facts

a) "Diagnosed at 13 years old with Complex Regional Pain Syndrome, formerly known as Reflex Sympathetic Dystrophy (CRPS/RSD), an incurable and progressive chronic pain disease of the sympathetic nervous system, she lives every day in severe pain."

b) "CRPS/RSD is ranked as the most painful form of chronic pain that exists today by the McGill Pain Index."

c) "The United Nations Universal Declaration of Human Rights states in Article 5, "No one shall be subjected to torture or to cruel, inhuman or degrading treatment or punishment."

d) "Medical doctors in the United States take the Hippocratic Oath that states, "I will follow that system of regimen which, according to my ability and judgment, I consider for the benefit of my patients, and abstain from whatever is deleterious and mischievous."

Reasoning

a) "Yet the government, in a short-sighted effort to combat widespread opioid abuse, wants to take Madison's lifeline away."

b) "Our military does the best it can to minimize collateral damage on the innocent and unintended targets even if it means sparing the intended targets."

c) "What we are not shown are the millions of patients in the USA alone who, but for their opioid medication, would be left in constant and excruciating pain."

d) "Although these numbers are tragic, we would not want to see the physicians associated with these prescriptions threatened."

Stylistic Elements

a) **Fragments:** "None of them worked," "And it should be that way," "But there will be collateral damage to this," etc.

b) **Impactful Phrasing:** "lifeline," "collateral damage," "unspeakable pain," "tragic," etc.

c) **Rhetorical Questions:** "How can we be in direct conflict to both the Declaration of Human Rights and the Hippocratic Oath, and cause immense suffering to those of us who are in chronic, incurable pain? How can we reconcile the fact that, as a country, we can show compassion and lend assistance to refugees, and send food and medical aid to Third World countries, yet allow our family and friends to be denied the medication they need to survive?" Etc.

Persuasive Elements

a) Emotional appeal: "With the advice of numerous physicians over the last 13 years, we have tried every possible remedy and every possible treatment. None of them worked. So many days, I can only hold her in my arms as she cries in agony. The only thing that eases her suffering slightly is her prescription of opioid medication." Etc.

b) Comparisons: "Our military does the best it can to minimize collateral damage on the innocent and unintended targets even if it means sparing the intended targets." "Sadly, there are thousands of people who die from the over-the-counter drug ibuprofen every year." Etc.

c) Credibility: First-hand experience with a chronic pain sufferer, quotes from the Declaration of Human Rights and the Hippocratic Oath, etc.

Thoroughly read through the entire text given, paying special attention to key points. You will only have time for one full read through. Key points will be quickly exposed through a thesis-like statement and topic sentences. An author's thesis statement most often appears in the introductory paragraph and sometimes title. Lemmon's thesis, in not as clear words, appears after the introduction of her daughter, and then again more clearly towards the end of the article.

Lemmon's Thesis:

Yet the government, in a short-sighted effort to combat widespread opioid abuse, wants to take Madison's lifeline away. She, along with many others in her situation, are apparently considered collateral damage. Collateral damage is not acceptable.

Taking away their right to be treated for their pain is the real opioid crisis.

10

Lemmon's Topic sentences:

Topic sentences are the first sentence of every paragraph.

"My 26-year-old daughter, Madison, is an extremely intelligent, articulate, creative and beautiful young woman."

"CRPS/RSD is ranked as the most painful form of chronic pain that exists today by the McGill Pain Index."

"Collateral damage is not acceptable."

"Why, then, is our government inflicting cruel and unusual punishment for innocent victims here at home?"

Etc.

The author's key points will be the structure that your own key points mimic. In this case, Lemmon's key points are undeserved pain, conflicting government policies, and a lack of government reasoning. Analyze these points for persuasive techniques, and you have emotional appeal, comparisons, and rhetorical questions. These three things are the "how" that the sample essay chooses to focus on, but Lemmon uses other techniques (like those examples given above), as well, to persuade her audience. No two essays will be alike as you and your peers will analyze Lemmon's work through a personal lens.

Create a clear and concise thesis that states the author's persuasive techniques.

Sample essay's thesis: *She supports her claim by making emotional appeals, drawing relatable comparisons, and asking rhetorical questions.*

For detailed analysis, these techniques could reasonably be a list of 2-4 (3, in the sample essay's case). One essay style is to focus each body paragraph on one of those techniques. Another style would be to summarize like techniques in paragraphs together. Paraphrase and quote a few specific lines from the text that support your analysis. Keep any quotes used relatively short. Make sure to always surround a quote with your own words. Introduce the quote, include the quote, and then clearly explain why this quote shows the author's persuasive technique. The essay should be mostly your words, not the authors.

Conclude your essay by pointing out the author's intentions, along with their specific audience. Avoid merely restating your thesis.

Sample essay: *She advocates for those with chronic pain disease to have access to the medications they need, and if policy-makers or those with a voice, are reading her article, they should recognize that this policy that promotes pain and contradicts other procedures just does n't make sense.*

10

Answer Sheet

Use a No. 2 pencil. Begin your essay on this page. If you need more space, continue on the next page.

_____

_____

_____

_____

_____

_____

_____

_____

10

10

Sample Essay

The American government is cracking down on drug abuse and it's targeting the opioid crisis. According to Kindly Lemmon, new regulations won't be all good. Lemmon argues that taking away opioids for chronic pain sufferers is the real opioid crisis. She supports her claim by making emotional appeals, drawing relatable comparisons, and asking rhetorical questions.

Lemmon uses emotional appeals to make the suffering of those with chronic pain disease real for readers. She relays the pain her own daughter experiences with Complex Regional Pain Syndrome where "she lives every day in severe pain". In fact, there are some days her daughter is inconsolable, and all Lemmon can do is hold her "as she cries in agony". Lemmon tells this first-hand and personal experience to appeal to the reader's humanity. She hopes that policy-makers and readers with influence, will recognize that not all opioid users are abusers but are in real need of relief, and not of their own choice. Lemmon shows the reader again when she highlights that her daughter is not the only one; there are millions who suffer from chronic pain and who without opioids would experience "unspeakable pain and even death". Lemmon aims to get the reader to feel again, the uncomfortable fact that innocent people shouldn't have to suffer if there is a working medication.

When explaining the government's new war against opioids, Lemmon makes comparisons to other American procedures that contradict such a zero-tolerance policy. Lemmon's daughter would be "collateral damage" in the war against opioids, but to Lemmon, that's not fair. She compares the military to such a policy, pointing out that even they make major efforts to avoid collateral damage. She aims to have the reader realize that if a military target can be forgotten in favor of saving innocents, the government can do the same for opioids and chronic pain sufferers. In another comparison, Lemmon points out the direct contradiction of the United Nations Universal Declaration of Human Rights and the Hippocratic Oath. She hopes to make the hypocrisy clear to her audience; you can't state that no one should be subject to torture and make doctors swear to treat patients to their benefit, at the same time. That is, not if you're going to torture those with chronic pain disease. Her last paragraph makes one last large comparison to over-the-counter drugs. Plenty of people die from those, but they are not going to be regulated like opioids. This aims to be an even more relatable comparison for the reader because most people have Advil, Ibuprofen, Tylenol, etc., in their homes.

Stylistically, Lemmon turns to rhetorical questions for aid in her argument against the government's opioid movement. Her rhetorical questions force the reader to consider the baffling non-answers that come from her explained comparisons. In correlation to her military comparison, Lemmon asks, "Why, then, is our government inflicting cruel and unusual punishment for innocent victims here at home?" Lemmon hopes her audience recognizes that there is no valid answer to this question, and she suggests that if the reader can't find an answer, the government has no logical right. Similarly, she asks how the Declaration of Human Rights and the Hippocratic Oath can be in direct conflict, and how can we give aid to third world countries when we cause our own to suffer? Lemmon asks these questions because it should be clear that there is no excuse for the harsh stance the government has taken against opioids for not just abusers, but for all.

Too many deaths occur because of over-the-counter and prescription drugs every year. Death, though, would also occur without those drugs, according to Lemmon. She advocates for those with chronic pain disease to have access to the medications they need, and if policy-makers or those with a voice, are reading her article, they should recognize that this policy that promotes pain and contradicts other procedures just doesn't make sense.

10

Prompt

••

As you read the passage below, consider how Wek uses

❑ evidence, such as facts or examples, to support claims.

❑ reasoning to develop ideas and to connect claims and evidence.

❑ stylistic or persuasive elements, such as word choice or appeals to emotion, to add power to the ideas expressed.

••

Adapted from Alek Wek, "Give refugee children something that cannot be taken away -- an education" ©2017 by CNN. Originally published September 12, 2017.

1. I was 14 when I became a refugee.

2. As civil war tore through my village, I lost friends and neighbors. I could no longer go to school. And eventually, I couldn't even leave the house.

3. When the danger became too great my family and I had to flee - leaving behind our home, almost all of our possessions and our entire way of life.

4. Never again would I roam the village with my schoolmates after lessons, snacking on mangoes, wandering out to check on my mother's cows or running up the big hill nearby to gaze at the airplanes passing overhead.

5. Never again would my mother's main worry in life be whether or not I would be back in time for supper. Never again would my family, all 11 of us, be together under one roof. That period of my life is scarred by deep, life-changing loss.

6. In the face of this upheaval, I held fast to something my father had told me. "You can lose almost everything," he said, "but you can never lose your education."

7. If, as a refugee, education was the one thing that could not be taken away from me, then I was going to immerse myself in learning. And that is exactly what I did.

8. The moment came when my mother saw the chance to send me and one of my sisters to London. I had mixed feelings about this - I was devastated to be separated from her, but I was relieved to finally reach safety. I had endured a great deal, I was still having nightmares and sudden noises terrified me - even the slamming of a door.

9. Education became my refuge. It gave me stability and security when everything else seemed to have fallen apart. I had always loved school but now, having missed several years, I saw it through new eyes - something not to be treated lightly, and certainly not to be taken for granted. Now it was not just about learning for the love of learning; now it was essential to finding my own way forward.

10. I remember well my first day of school in London. I was intimidated and afraid - I looked different from my fellow students, I couldn't speak English and I got called a whole host of names. But I was grateful to be there, even so. And with my father's words driving me on, I gave it everything I had.

11. Education was empowering. My confidence and self-esteem rose and at long last I could see a small light at the end of what had been a long and very dark tunnel. Education gave me not just the skills I needed to navigate what ended up being a very demanding career in fashion, but it also gave me hope and optimism. It gave me the space to explore how to be the best person I could be.

12. Every child deserves such an opportunity to be empowered - indeed, it is every child's right. For millions of refugee children and adolescents, however, it does not exist. Overall, less than half of school-age refugee children attend school; those hoping for a secondary or tertiary education see their chances shrink with each passing year. The older a refugee gets, the more likely it is that access to the classroom will be denied.

13. There is a clear gap in opportunity for refugee and non-refugee children, and we must do everything in our power to close it. This means investing in classrooms and teachers for refugees. It means giving them access to appropriate material. It also means supporting girls so that they have the same opportunities as boys. The world has much to lose if it allows whole generations of refugees to grow up uneducated and alienated.

14. As a goodwill ambassador for UNHCR - the UN refugee agency - I have met many young refugees who yearned to get an education, just as I did. I have met children who walk three hours just to get to school. I know what learning means to them because I know what it meant to me.

15. Today, my father's voice, still ringing in my ears, inspires me to advocate for access to education on behalf of all those who are left behind. It is my hope that we unite as a global community and prioritize education, that we see an increase in funding and access to national systems, that we see all refugee children enjoying their right to education and thereby finding dignity, passion and the bright futures they deserve.

11

Write an essay in which you explain how Wek builds an argument to persuade her audience that refugee children need equal access to education. In your essay, analyze how Wek uses one or more of the features listed above (or features of your own choice) to strengthen the logic and persuasiveness of her argument. Be sure that your analysis focuses on the most relevant features of the passage.

Your essay should not explain whether you agree with Wek's claims, but rather explain how the author builds an argument to persuade her audience.

Pre-Essay Writing

Read the essay prompt before you read the provided text. Make sure you have a firm grasp on what the prompt is asking you to analyze in your essay. In this case, the prompt specifically says, "explain how Wek builds an argument to persuade her audience that refugee children need equal access to education". A keyword here is "how". How does Wek persuade her audience? Recall the bullet points already given to you, asking you to notice evidence such as facts, statistics, or reliable experience, reasoning that connects ideas through logic and explanation, and stylistic or persuasive elements such as word choice, emotional appeal, building credibility, etc. Wek's techniques will show up in her body paragraphs. As you read, take note of Wek's use of these things and begin to mentally map out your essay.

Some examples from Wek's text:

Facts

a) "I was 14 when I became a refugee."

b) "Overall, less than half of school-age refugee children attend school; those hoping for a secondary or tertiary education see their chances shrink with each passing year."

c) "The older a refugee gets, the more likely it is that access to the classroom will be denied."

d) "As a goodwill ambassador for UNHCR - the UN refugee agency - I have met many young refugees who yearned to get an education, just as I did."

Reasoning

a) "If, as a refugee, education was the one thing that could not be taken away from me, then I was going to immerse myself in learning."

b) "Education gave me not just the skills I needed to navigate what ended up being a very demanding career in fashion, but it also gave me hope and optimism."

c) "The world has much to lose if it allows whole generations of refugees to grow up uneducated and alien-ated."

d) "There is a clear gap in opportunity for refugee and non-refugee children, and we must do everything in our power to close it."

Stylistic Elements

a) Repetition: "Never again," "Now," "Gave," etc.

b) Positive word association: "empowering," "driving," "enjoying," "finding," etc.

c) Clear transitions: "In the face of this upheaval," "Today," "If, as a refugee," "Overall," etc.

Persuasive Elements

a) Emotional appeal: "The moment came when my mother saw the chance to send me and one of my sisters to London. I had mixed feelings about this -- I was devastated to be separated from her, but I was relieved to finally reach safety. I had endured a great deal, I was still having nightmares and sudden noises terrified me - even the slamming of a door." Etc.

b) Credibility: First-hand experience as a refugee, UN Ambassador, educated, etc.

c) Relatability: "Every child deserves such an opportunity to be empowered - indeed, it is every child's right." Etc.

Thoroughly read through the entire text given, paying special attention to key points. You will only have time for one full read through. Key points will be quickly exposed through a thesis-like statement and topic sentences. An author's thesis statement most often appears in the introductory paragraph and sometimes title. Wek's thesis appears in the title and after she has given the background of her own experience.

Wek's Thesis:

There is a clear gap in opportunity for refugee and non-refugee children, and we must do everything in our power to close it.

Wek's Topic sentences:

Topic sentences are the first sentence of every paragraph.

"As civil war tore through my village, I lost friends and neighbors."

"The moment came when my mother saw the chance to send me and one of my sisters to London."

"Education became my refuge."

"Every child deserves such an opportunity to be empowered -- indeed, it is every child's right."

Etc.

The author's key points will be the structure that your own key points mimic. In this case, Wek's key points are the devastation refugee children experience, the hope they need, and the possible positive change available to them. Analyze these points for persuasive techniques, and you have emotional appeal, purposeful reasoning, and repetition. These three things are the "how" that the sample essay chooses to focus on, but Wek uses other techniques (like those examples given above), as well, to persuade her audience. No two essays will be alike as you and your peers will analyze Wek's work through a personal lens.

Create a clear and concise thesis that states the author's persuasive techniques.

Sample essay's thesis: *She supports her claims by appealing to audience emotions, displaying clear reasoning, and utilizing purposeful repetition.*

For detailed analysis, these techniques could reasonably be a list of 2-4 (3, in the sample essay's case). One essay style is to focus each body paragraph on one of those techniques. Another style would be to summarize like techniques in paragraphs together. Paraphrase and quote a few specific lines from the text that support your analysis. Keep any quotes used relatively short. Make sure to always surround a quote with your own words. Introduce the quote, include the quote, and then clearly explain why this quote shows the author's persuasive technique. The essay should be mostly your words, not the authors.

Conclude your essay by pointing out the author's intentions, along with their specific audience. Avoid merely restating your thesis.

Sample essay: *She hopes that those with the funds, connections, and a voice to help will do so. After taking them through an emotional journey, a track of logic, and a repeated message, Wek hopes readers will take the next step to help refugee children have a bright future.*

11

Answer Sheet

Use a No. 2 pencil. Begin your essay on this page. If you need more space, continue on the next page.

_____

_____

_____

_____

_____

_____

_____

_____

11

11

Sample Essay

Alek Wek speaks from a deeply personal place when she writes for CNN to explain the most important thing refugee children need. Wek argues that refugee children need equal access to education in order to thrive, the same access as non-refugee children. She supports her claims by appealing to audience emotions, displaying clear reasoning, and utilizing purposeful repetition.

For Alek Wek, the subject of refugee children is an emotional affair, and she aims to make it one for her readers, as well. Wek explains her own past as a child refugee, calling up painful memories and difficult circumstances. When she mentions the loss of her village, her friends, her school, and her house, Wek means to put the reader in her shoes. These are things that most readers can, but don't want to, imagine losing. She aims to make them imagine. She continues the story by going into detail about the pleasant life that she would no longer have, ending with, "That period of my life is scarred by deep, life-changing loss." Wek wants the reader to be clear on the tumult that refugee children go through: life-changing tumult. Ultimately, Wek ties her childhood back into an education. The yearning she felt for education is not unique. "I have met children who walk three hours just to get to school. I know what learning means to them because I know what it meant to me." Wek links the sympathy readers feel for refugees to the simple, and now seemingly privileged solution, of education.

Wek also makes a case for refugee education by displaying a clear process of reasoning. A driving idea in Wek's article is the indispensable nature of education. She quotes her father's logical advice, "'You can lose almost everything,' he said, 'but you can never lose your education.'" This speaks to the experience of all readers. Wek calls to reason that refugees may lose every worldly possession, but their knowledge will follow them everywhere. Similarly, CNN readers know that education is a right in America, but as Wek points out, refugees don't have access to that education. Americans may take their education for granted then, thinking education isn't that special. She states that for "millions of refugee children," education would, in fact, be special. It would be a source of opportunity, dignity, and empowerment. Wek hopes to show a clear and reasonable deficit to the reader.

Lastly, Wek writes with stylized repetition to reinforce the impact of material loss and redemptive education. When describing the loss of her comfortable childhood, Wek repeats the phrase, "Never again". "Never again" would she see her schoolmates in the village; "Never again" would her mother worry about on-time supper arrivals; "Never again" would her family live all together. Wek's repetition works like a blow taken to the heart of the reader. Her repetition of the word "now" shows a pleasant turn of events. "Now it was not just about learning for the love of learning; now it was essential to finding my own way forward." Wek's purposeful repetition here reinforces the positive impact education had on her life. Similarly, she repeats "gave" to list all that education can do for a refugee. It gives skills, hope and optimism, and space to explore who you are. These are positive changes that Wek hopes to have the reader recognize and support.

There are a lot of resources that refugee children need, but education, according to Wek, is not only the most useful, it's the most important. She hopes that those with the funds, connections, and a voice to help will do so. After taking them through an emotional journey, a track of logic, and a reinforced message, Wek hopes readers will take the next step to help refugee children have a bright future.

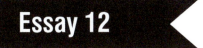

Prompt

As you read the passage below, consider how Upton uses

- ❏ evidence, such as facts or examples, to support claims.

- ❏ reasoning to develop ideas and to connect claims and evidence.

- ❏ stylistic or persuasive elements, such as word choice or appeals to emotion, to add power to the ideas expressed.

Adapted from Simon Upton, "Air Pollution's True Costs" ©2016 by Project Syndicate. Originally published August 16, 2016.

1. Air pollution takes years off people's lives. It causes substantial pain and suffering, among adults and children alike. And it damages food production, at a time when we need to feed more people than ever. This is not just an economic issue; it is a moral one.

2. Air pollution can be produced both outdoors and indoors. For the poorest families, indoor smog from coal- or dung-fired cooking stoves is typically the more serious problem. As economies develop and start to electrify, motorize, and urbanize, outdoor air pollution becomes the bigger issue.

3. Cleaner technologies are available, with the potential to improve air quality considerably. But policymakers tend to focus myopically on the costs of action, rather than the costs of inaction. With economic growth and rising energy demand set to fuel a steady rise in emissions of air pollutants and rapidly rising concentrations of particulate matter (PM) and ozone in the coming decades, this approach is untenable.

4. A new OECD report, The Economic Consequences of Outdoor Air Pollution, estimates that outdoor air pollution will cause 6-9 million premature deaths annually by 2060, compared to three million in 2010. That is equivalent to a person dying every 4-5 seconds. Cumulatively, more than 200 million people will die prematurely in the next 45 years as a result of air pollution.

5. There will also be more pollution-related illness. New cases of bronchitis in children aged 6-12 are forecast to soar to 36 million per year by 2060, from 12 million today. For adults, we predict ten million new cases per year by 2060, up from 3.5 million today. Children are also being increasingly affected by asthma. All of this will translate into more pollution-related hospital admissions, projected to rise to 11 million in 2060, from 3.6 million in 2010.

6. These health problems will be concentrated in densely populated areas with high PM concentrations, especially cities in China and India. In per capita terms, mortality is also set to reach high levels in Eastern

Europe, the Caucasus region, and other parts of Asia, such as South Korea, where aging populations are highly vulnerable to air pollution.

7. The impact of air pollution is often discussed in dollar terms. By 2060, 3.75 billion working days per year could be lost due to the adverse health effects of dirty air - what economists call the "disutility of illness." The direct market impact of this pollution in terms of lower worker productivity, higher health spending, and lower crop yields, could exceed 1% of GDP, or $2.6 trillion, annually by 2060.

8. Massive as they are, however, the dollar figures do not reflect the true costs of air pollution. Premature deaths from breathing in small particles and toxic gases, and the pain and suffering from respiratory and cardiovascular diseases, do not have a market price. Nor does the experience of constantly inhaling foul-smelling air or forcing your child to wear a face mask just to play outside. These burdens weigh far more heavily on people than any price tag can represent.

9. Nonetheless, the truth remains that policymakers tend to respond more to hard figures than to abstract experiences. So, the OECD examined myriad economic studies on air pollution to quantify what people's health is worth to them.

10. On average, individuals would be prepared to pay around $30 to reduce their annual risk of dying prematurely by one in 100,000. Using well-established techniques, these "willingness-to-pay" figures were converted into an overall value of premature deaths caused by outdoor air pollution, as illustrated, for example, in the OECD's Mortality Risk Valuation in Environment, Health and Transport Policies.

11. By that measure, the global cost of premature deaths caused by outdoor air pollution would reach a staggering $18-25 trillion a year by 2060. Arguably, this is not "real" money, as the costs are not related to any market transactions. But it does reflect the value people put on their very real lives – and the value they would put on policies that would help to delay their very real deaths.

12. It is time for governments to stop fussing about the costs of efforts to limit air pollution and start worrying about the much larger costs of allowing it to continue unchecked. Their citizens' lives are in their hands.

12

Write an essay in which you explain how Upton builds an argument to persuade his audience that air pollution is a serious threat to human life. In your essay, analyze how Upton uses one or more of the features listed above (or features of your own choice) to strengthen the logic and persuasiveness of his argument. Be sure that your analysis focuses on the most relevant features of the passage.

Your essay should not explain whether you agree with Upton's claims, but rather explain how the author builds an argument to persuade his audience.

Pre-Essay Writing

Read the essay prompt before you read the provided text. Make sure you have a firm grasp on what the prompt is asking you to analyze in your essay. In this case, the prompt specifically says, "explain how Upton builds an argument to persuade his audience that air pollution is a serious threat to human life". A keyword here is "how". How does Upton persuade his audience? Recall the bullet points already given to you, asking you to notice evidence such as facts, statistics, or reliable experience, reasoning that connects ideas through logic and explanation, and stylistic or persuasive elements such as word choice, emotional appeal, building credibility, etc. Upton's techniques will show up in his body paragraphs. As you read, take note of Upton's use of these things and begin to mentally map out your essay.

Some examples from Upton's text:

Facts

a) "For the poorest families, indoor smog from coal- or dung-fired cooking stoves is typically the more serious problem."

b) "As economies develop and start to electrify, motorize, and urbanize, outdoor air pollution becomes the bigger issue."

c) "These health problems will be concentrated in densely populated areas with high PM concentrations, especially cities in China and India."

d) "So, the OECD examined myriad economic studies on air pollution to quantify what people's health is worth to them."

Statistics

a) "A new OECD report, The Economic Consequences of Outdoor Air Pollution, estimates that outdoor air pollution will cause 6-9 million premature deaths annually by 2060, compared to three million in 2010."

b) "Cumulatively, more than 200 million people will die prematurely in the next 45 years as a result of air pollution."

c) "New cases of bronchitis in children aged 6-12 are forecast to soar to 36 million per year by 2060, from 12 million today. For adults, we predict ten million new cases per year by 2060, up from 3.5 million today."

d) "All of this will translate into more pollution-related hospital admissions, projected to rise to 11 million in 2060, from 3.6 million in 2010."

Reasoning

a) "That is equivalent to a person dying every 4-5 seconds."

b) "Massive as they are, however, the dollar figures do not reflect the true costs of air pollution."

c) "But policymakers tend to focus myopically on the costs of action, rather than the costs of inaction. With economic growth and rising energy demand set to fuel a steady rise in emissions of air pollutants and rapidly rising concentrations of particulate matter (PM) and ozone in the coming decades, this approach is untenable."

d) "Arguably, this is not "real" money, as the costs are not related to any market transactions. But it does reflect the value people put on their very real lives – and the value they would put on policies that would help to delay their very real deaths.

Stylistic Elements

a) Creating urgency: "staggering $18-25 trillion a year by 2060," "6-9 million premature deaths annually by 2060, compared to three million in 2010".

b) Strong word choice: "myopically," "untenable," "burden," "staggering," etc.

c) Clear transitions: "Moreover," "Nonetheless," "On average," etc.

Persuasive Elements

a) Emotional appeal: "Premature deaths from breathing in small particles and toxic gases, and the pain and suffering from respiratory and cardiovascular diseases, do not have a market price. Nor does the experience of constantly inhaling foul-smelling air or forcing your child to wear a face mask just to play outside."

b) Trustworthy: "A new OECD report, The Economic Consequences of Outdoor Air Pollution, estimates that outdoor air pollution will cause 6-9 million premature deaths annually by 2060, compared to three million in 2010."

c) Credibility: "This is not just an economic issue; it is a moral one."

12

Thoroughly read through the entire text given, paying special attention to key points. You will only have time for one full read through. Key points will be quickly exposed through a thesis-like statement and topic sentences. An author's thesis statement most often appears in the introductory paragraph.

Upton's Thesis:

Air pollution takes years off people's lives. It causes substantial pain and suffering, among adults and children alike. And it damages food production, at a time when we need to feed more people than ever. This is not just an economic issue; it is a moral one.

Upton's Topic sentences:

Topic sentences are the first sentence of every paragraph.

"A new OECD report...estimates that outdoor air pollution will cause 6-9 million premature deaths annually by 2060, compared to three million in 2010."

"There will also be more pollution-related illness."

"The impact of air pollution is often discussed in dollar terms."

"Massive as they are, however, the dollar figures do not reflect the true costs of air pollution."

Etc.

The author's key points will be the structure that your own key points mimic. In this case, Upton's key points are rising death tolls, a decrease in life quality, and a struggle for change. Analyze these points for persuasive techniques, and you have statistics, emotional appeal, and a sense of urgency. These three things are the "how" that the sample essay chooses to focus on, but Upton uses other techniques (like those examples given above), as well, to persuade his audience. No two essays will be alike as you and your peers will analyze Upton's work through a personal lens.

Create a clear and concise thesis that states the author's persuasive techniques.

Sample essay's thesis: *Upton supports this claim by sharing shocking statistics, appealing to emotions, and creating a sense of urgency, especially for policymakers.*

For detailed analysis, these techniques could reasonably be a list of 2-4 (3, in the sample essay's case). One essay style is to focus each body paragraph on one of those techniques. Another style would be to summarize like techniques in paragraphs together. Paraphrase and quote a few specific lines from the text that support your analysis. Keep any quotes used relatively short. Make sure to always surround a quote with your own words. Introduce the quote, include the quote, and then clearly explain why this quote shows the author's persuasive technique. The essay should be mostly your words, not the authors.

Conclude your essay by pointing out the author's intentions, along with their specific audience. Avoid merely restating your thesis.

Sample essay: *Simon Upton calls out big policymakers in government positions to put money towards minimizing air pollution. If they wait too long, the high price they don't want to pay will only increase, a price that will include more and more human lives.*

Answer Sheet

Use a No. 2 pencil. Begin your essay on this page. If you need more space, continue on the next page.

12

12

12

Sample Essay

With an ever increasingly urban world, air pollution becomes an issue of discussion. Writer Simon Upton argues that air pollution is not only a bigger problem than most think, but also an issue that puts your very own life at stake. Upton supports this claim by sharing shocking statistics, appealing to emotions, and creating a sense of urgency, especially for policymakers.

Upton uses credible statistics to show the staggering numbers associated with air pollution. No matter how he categorizes them, the number of deaths, the number of illnesses, the number of money losses, etc., the numbers speak volumes of air pollution's impact. He references The Economic Consequences of Outdoor Air Pollution as estimating "that outdoor air pollution will cause 6-9 million premature deaths annually by 2060, compared to three million in 2010. That is equivalent to a person dying every 4-5 seconds". Upton's breakdown of the OECD's finding to seconds makes the numbers feel more real to the audience. He achieves this again when he translates air pollution side effects to something else people care about: money. "By 2060, 3.75 billion working days per year could be lost due to the adverse health effects of dirty air - what economists call the 'disutility of illness.'" On the flip side, people are willing to pay money now to reduce their own risk of death, amounts that add up to "$18-25 trillion a year by 2060", to be exact. There is a staggering amount of money to be spent in consequence of air pollution; Upton uses these numbers to shock his audience. If mortality rates don't scare them, maybe money spent before mortality, will.

Where statistics might fail, Upton turns to emotions in order to support his claim. He points out to the audience that numbers and statistics seem to miss the sad details of air pollution's danger. "Premature deaths from breathing in small particles and toxic gases, and the pain and suffering from respiratory and cardiovascular diseases, do not have a market price." It's even harder to ignore the threat of air pollution when Upton continues to paint a picture of foul air and constant face masks. He implies that this is a life no one wants to lead. All of these things would reduce our quality of life and are more important than a "price tag".

Lastly, Upton makes the audience feel the urgency of air pollution's threat by comparing the state of 2010 or today to the state of 2060. 50 more years is still in the lifetime of most people reading Upton's argument, but what a difference 50 years seems to make. "New cases of bronchitis in children aged 6-12 are forecast to soar to 36 million per year by 2060, from 12 million today." Child bronchitis cases will triple in such a short amount of time. Adding to the already mentioned rising risks, Upton states, "For adults, we predict ten million new cases per year by 2060, up from 3.5 million today." It's clear that Upton feels like a solution to the air quality issue needs to be implemented now, rather than later.

While many people know that air pollution is a problem, not much is being done to prevent it. Simon Upton calls out big policymakers in government positions to put money towards minimizing air pollution. If they wait too long, the high price they don't want to pay will only increase, a price that will include more and more human lives.

Essay 13

Prompt

As you read the passage below, consider how Garfield uses

❑ evidence, such as facts or examples, to support claims.

❑ reasoning to develop ideas and to connect claims and evidence.

❑ stylistic or persuasive elements, such as word choice or appeals to emotion, to add power to the ideas expressed.

Adapted from Charles Garfield, "You know 'thoughts and prayers' during a crisis aren't enough. Here's how to really be helpful" ©2017 by Los Angeles Times. Originally published October 24, 2017.

1. It's been one endless, exhausting "thoughts and prayers" season - a mass shooting, coast-to-coast disasters, losses of lives and homes and history, along with the steady drumbeat of "everyday" human frailties. A childhood friend just emailed with his news: lung cancer, metastasized, and a son diagnosed with acute lymphoma.

2. Death seems too close. Darkness falls. "Thoughts and prayers," we say. "Sending you and you and you our thoughts and prayers," even as we realize it's not enough. For nearly 50 years, I've helped people face death and illness, and I've come to see that what works at a bedside can make a difference in all manner of crises.

3. I saw the power of compassion early in my career as a psychologist on the cancer ward at the UC San Francisco Medical Center. Most of the patients there had dire prognoses, and I quickly discovered that whatever counseling I could offer paled next to the effect of simply being present. I sat with people whose friends and relatives were too afraid to visit, not sure what to do or say when a father or co-worker or neighbor was gravely ill. Sometimes I was the only one other than a nurse or cleaning person who shared a patient's final days.

4. In 1974, I founded Shanti Project to train ordinary people to visit and serve those at the end of their lives. When the AIDS crisis descended on San Francisco in the 1980s, we stayed with the ill and dying, comforted them and treated them as friends, not victims. Compassion was our baseline - being with people's suffering. We had no cures, but we helped many feel whole.

5. We discovered compassion is anything but abstract. It can be taught and practiced. Three basic skills make a sound protocol for any crisis, whether we've just learned a friend is dying or we're simply Americans in 2017, searching for ways to bridge divides, recover from disaster, heal abuse or summon the resilience to go

13

on.

6. The first skill is deep listening - we call it listening from the heart. This starts with looking the other person in the eye - making real contact - and then quieting the thoughts in your mind as you focus on responses to an open-ended question such as, "How are you doing?" or "How do you feel about what's going on?"

7. We encourage volunteers to be still, noticing when they drift away from listening. The idea is to keep returning to the moment, making eye contact again, directing one's attention to the other person's words, silences and nonverbal cues. Stay quiet, be willing to be moved by what you hear. Those in crisis need to know their experience matters. If you can just do one thing, listen in this manner.

8. Then speak from the heart. The most important thing to convey is, "I'm in this with you." What those in crisis want most is not to be alone with their fear and confusion. Push aside the temptation to rush to the rescue and impose solutions. Say things like: "How can we handle this together?" "What do you think we should do next?" or "Here's what makes sense to me. Does it make sense to you?" Partnership is far more meaningful than taking charge. As you speak, keep listening. The other person is the expert on his or her experience and needs.

9. Finally, act with, not for, the other person. When there's agreement on what to do next, make a statement of collaboration: "I will join with you as best I can to make that happen." It's partnership that counts.

10. If you have friends or family coping in the aftermath of California's wildfires, being a partner in someone's recovery might involve making offers like, "I can research how to get FEMA aid (or replace a driver's license, or find out long-term car rental rates), and let you know what I find that makes the most sense to me." Send a gift card to a store with many options, rather than a box of food. Or ask, "Would it be helpful if I came over? We can do some of this together." Action rooted in empathy is qualitatively different from swooping in and doing "what needs to be done."

11. Thoughts and prayers are important. I don't discount them. Sending money to aid agencies is essential and can do tremendous good. But empathy and compassion - seeing others as your equal, deeply imagining what they are going through - creates far deeper levels of support, relief and change. If you long to help, you'll be most effective when you concretely demonstrate, "We're in it together. I'm with you for the long run."

13

Write an essay in which you explain how Garfield builds an argument to persuade his audience that people need to stop relying solely on thoughts and prayers and actually act. In your essay, analyze how Garfield uses one or more of the features listed above (or features of your own choice) to strengthen the logic and persuasiveness of his argument. Be sure that your analysis focuses on the most relevant features of the passage.

Your essay should not explain whether you agree with Garfield's claims, but rather explain how the author builds an argument to persuade his audience.

Pre-Essay Writing

Read the essay prompt before you read the provided text. Make sure you have a firm grasp on what the prompt is asking you to analyze in your essay. In this case, the prompt specifically says, "explain how Garfield builds an argument to persuade his audience that people need to stop relying on thoughts and prayers and actually act". A keyword here is "how". How does Garfield persuade his audience? Recall the bullet points already given to you, asking you to notice evidence such as facts, statistics, or reliable experience, reasoning that connects ideas through logic and explanation, and stylistic or persuasive elements such as word choice, emotional appeal, building credibility, etc. Garfield's techniques will show up in his body paragraphs. As you read, take note of Garfield's use of these things and begin to mentally map out your essay.

Some examples from Garfield's text:

Facts

a) "I saw the power of compassion early in my career as a psychologist on the cancer ward at the UC San Francisco Medical Center."

b) "In 1974, I founded Shanti Project to train ordinary people to visit and serve those at the end of their lives."

c) "When the AIDS crisis descended on San Francisco in the 1980s, we stayed with the ill and dying, comforted them and treated them as friends, not victims."

d) "For nearly 50 years, I've helped people face death and illness, and I've come to see that what works at a bedside can make a difference in all manner of crises."

Reasoning

a) "We discovered compassion is anything but abstract. It can be taught and practiced."

13

b) "Those in crisis need to know their experience matters."

c) "What those in crisis want most is not to be alone with their fear and confusion."

d) "Send a gift card to a store with many options, rather than a box of food."

Stylistic Elements

a) Fragments: "Darkness falls. "Thoughts and prayers," we say. "Sending you and you and you our thoughts and prayers," even as we realize it's not enough."

b) Negative descriptors: "dire prognosis," "human frailties," "final days," etc.

c) Actionable instructions: "being present," "being with people," "be still," "be willing," "be moved," "being a partner," "be most effective…"

Persuasive Elements

a) Emotional appeal: "Most of the patients there had dire prognoses, and I quickly discovered that whatever counseling I could offer paled next to the effect of simply being present. I sat with people whose friends and relatives were too afraid to visit, not sure what to do or say when a father or co-worker or neighbor was gravely ill. Sometimes I was the only one other than a nurse or cleaning person who shared a patient's final days." Etc.

b) Logical steps: "The first skill is deep listening…" "Then speak from the heart." "Finally, act with, not for, the other person." Etc.

c) Credibility: "I saw the power of compassion early in my career as a psychologist on the cancer ward at the UC San Francisco Medical Center." Etc.

Thoroughly read through the entire text given, paying special attention to key points. You will only have time for one full read through. Key points will be quickly exposed through a thesis-like statement and topic sentences. An author's thesis statement most often appears in the introductory paragraph and/or title. Garfield's thesis appears in his title and in his second paragraph after a bit of introduction.

Garfield's Thesis:

"Sending you and you and you our thoughts and prayers," even as we realize it's not enough.

Garfield's Topic sentences:

Topic sentences are the first sentence of every paragraph.

"It's been one endless, exhausting "thoughts and prayers" season - a mass shooting, coast-to-coast disasters, losses of

lives and homes and history, along with the steady drumbeat of "everyday" human frailties."

"Death seems too close."

"I saw the power of compassion early in my career as a psychologist on the cancer ward at the UC San Francisco Medical Center."

"In 1974, I founded Shanti Project to train ordinary people to visit and serve those at the end of their lives."

Etc.

The author's key points will be the structure that your own key points mimic. In this case, Garfield's key points are rising frequent suffering, lack of how to help, experts who have better ways. Analyze these points for persuasive techniques, and you have emotional appeal, logic, and credibility. These three things are the "how" that the sample essay chooses to focus on, but Garfield uses other techniques (like those examples given above), as well, to persuade his audience. No two essays will be alike as you and your peers will analyze Garfield's work through a personal lens.

Create a clear and concise thesis that states the author's persuasive techniques.

Sample essay's thesis: *He supports his claim by appealing to the reader's emotional side, sense of logical, and search for trust.*

For detailed analysis, these techniques could reasonably be a list of 2-4 (3, in the sample essay's case). One essay style is to focus each body paragraph on one of those techniques. Another style would be to summarize like techniques in paragraphs together. Paraphrase and quote a few specific lines from the text that support your analysis. Keep any quotes used relatively short. Make sure to always surround a quote with your own words. Introduce the quote, include the quote, and then clearly explain why this quote shows the author's persuasive technique. The essay should be mostly your words, not the authors.

Conclude your essay by pointing out the author's intentions, along with their specific audience. Avoid merely restating your thesis.

Sample essay: *It's easy to feel powerless in times of suffering, especially when that suffering is happening to someone else. Garfield, though, knows that no one is truly powerless. He shows the reader (everyone, really) that with your emotions, your sense of logic, and your trust in the experts, you can do more than ignore and more than thoughts and prayers, you can act and help.*

13

Answer Sheet

Use a No. 2 pencil. Begin your essay on this page. If you need more space, continue on the next page.

_____

_____

_____

_____

_____

_____

_____

_____

_____

_____

_____

_____

_____

_____

_____

_____

_____

_____

_____

_____

_____

_____

13

_____

_____

_____

_____

_____

_____

Sample Essay

In a time of tragedy and turmoil, it's hard to know how to help. Most people fall back on expressions of thoughts and prayers. According to Charles Garfield, though, people need to stop relying solely on thoughts and prayers and actually act. He supports his claim by appealing to the reader's emotional side, sense of logic, and need for trust.

Mass shootings, natural disasters, and loss of loved ones are all emotional things to begin with, so Garfield starts making his point there. During and after these events, Garfield explains, "Darkness falls. 'Thoughts and prayers,' we say." This use of fragments is a stylistic choice to make the reader feel the drama. The ending "We say" is also thrown in with a kind of skepticism. Suddenly, "thoughts and prayers" sound pretty weak in the face of "darkness". Garfield continues to build up the tragedy of these events with negative and sad descriptors like "dire prognosis," "human frailties," "final days". With words like these, he aims to make the reader feel dark, indeed. Then, he attaches a bit of the reader's guilt to these awful situations. Garfield describes people who don't really say or do anything when their coworkers or neighbors are ill, living in this darkness. The description of these absent helpers is meant to be a little too relatable. Garfield wants his reader to actually feel like the thoughts and prayers they've been offering aren't enough.

In case his readers aren't the emotional type, Garfield uses logic to support his claim, as well. Because thoughts and prayers aren't enough, there has to be better options. Garfield provides those options for the audience, and he provides them in a 3-step process. In his directions to first, listen deeply, second, speak from the heart, and third, act with the other person, he not only tells the reader what to do, but also gives ideas for what to say. Garfield gives clear and easy directions, so the reader truly has no excuse for not implementing them. Garfield also uses simple, actionable phrases throughout the article. He instructs the reader to "be present," "be with people," "be still," "be willing," "be moved," and "be a partner". Garfield's use of these straightforward statements shows the reader that helping doesn't have to be complicated, but it has to be action, and it has to be more than "thoughts and prayers". It should sound logical.

Lastly, Garfield reassures the reader that he's someone with an opinion they can trust. While Garfield is a human who has seen personal tragedy and an American who has seen national devastation, he has seen more human suffering than most. Garfield was a "psychologist on the cancer ward at the UC San Francisco Medical Center". He also founded the Shanti Project, a project that trains the everyman how to visit with people who are dying. Garfield points out his experience in an effort to show the reader that dealing with suffering is his expertise, and he truly knows what works best. He also builds his credibility by not totally discounting "thoughts and prayers". He recognizes the comfort that those sentiments often bring. He just feels like there's more. This recognition stops those readers who truly connect to prayer from getting offended by Garfield.

It's easy to feel powerless in times of suffering, especially when that suffering is happening to someone else. Garfield, though, knows that no one is truly powerless. He shows the reader (everyone, really) that with your emotions, your sense of logic, and your trust in the experts, you can do more than ignore and more than thoughts and prayers, you can act and help.

13

Essay 14

Prompt

As you read the passage below, consider how Obeidallah uses

- ❑ evidence, such as facts or examples, to support claims.

- ❑ reasoning to develop ideas and to connect claims and evidence.

- ❑ stylistic or persuasive elements, such as word choice or appeals to emotion, to add power to the ideas expressed.

Adapted from Dean Obeidallah, "Trump's beef with SNL is no laughing matter" ©2017 by CNN. Originally published October 17, 2016.

1. Nothing says Donald Trump has the judgment and temperament to be President of the United States like tweeting at 7:14 on Sunday morning that he thinks "Saturday Night Live" should be canceled.

2. But there was Trump, just 24 days before the election, composing yet another unhinged tweet as most Americans were still sleeping: "Watched 'Saturday Night Live' hit job on me. Time to retire the boring and unfunny show. Alec Baldwin portrayal stinks. Media rigging election!"

3. Apparently, Trump was upset with the way SNL depicted him in a sketch based on the second presidential debate. While the sketch mocked Hillary Clinton on numerous occasions for being too calculated and insincere, apparently that was not good enough for Trump.

4. Perhaps Trump was angered that one of the best moments of the sketch was when SNL highlighted Trump's hypocrisy concerning the recent sexual assault claims. Alec Baldwin, as Trump, demanded that the victims of Bill Clinton's alleged sexual misconduct "need to be respected and their voices need to be heard." But when Trump was asked about the women accusing him of sexual misconduct, he shot back: "They need to shut the hell up."

5. All kidding aside, Trump's tweet that "SNL" needs to be canceled because the show did a "hit job" on him should concern every American. We have a rich tradition of comedy shows skewering our politicians. I can't recall any President or presidential nominee responding to a TV show mocking him or her by saying it's time to take that show off the airwaves.

6. Although I have performed stand-up in the Middle East, where leaders have shared a similar sentiment. In fact, Egypt's Jon Stewart, Bassem Yourself, was arrested for mocking the then leader of Egypt and his TV show was ultimately canceled. But is that really a model we want to emulate in the United States?

7. Now, this is not the first time Trump has lashed out at comedians for jokes about him. When Seth Meyers

14

skewered Trump at the 2011 White House Correspondent's Dinner, Trump called Meyers "a stutterer."

8. But that was tame compared to the way he responded to Jon Stewart and Bill Maher. In the case of Stewart, who for years called out Trump for his outlandish behavior and comments, Trump tweeted that Stewart was "highly overrated" and a "total phony." And Trump's social media activity even bordered on anti-Semitic when he mocked Stewart by bizarrely tweeting out his real last name, "Leibowitz."

9. And in the case of Maher, Trump actually sued the comedian for $5 million. It was in response to a 2013 joke on "The Tonight Show," when Maher said he would donate $5 million to charity if Trump could prove he wasn't the "the spawn of his mother having sex with an orangutan." This joke was in response to Trump's offer of the same amount if President Barack Obama would release his college transcripts. Trump later withdraw the lawsuit, but the message was clear: Mock me, and I might sue you.

10. Couple all this with Trump's calls during this campaign to change the libel laws to make it easier for him to sue media outlets who unfairly criticize him, and this is no laughing matter.

11. Would a President Trump use the apparatus of the federal government - such as the Federal Communications Commission - to intimidate comedians and dissuade them from mocking him? Yes, I know we have a First Amendment, but alarmingly I bet there are Trump supporters who would go along with anything Trump asks for, even if it was flat out unconstitutional. (Trump has bragged as much, claiming he could shoot someone on Fifth Avenue and his supporters would stand with him.)

12. And even if Trump never went that far, his attacks on "SNL" could have a chilling effect. Comedians, fearing both his social media presence and the wrath of the millions of his Twitter followers, could remain silent on all Trump-related matters.

13. I pray "SNL" will not let Trump's tweet deter it in its comedic mission. In fact, I hope that between now and Election Day, "SNL," late-night hosts and comedians nationwide will transform Trump into the punchline he was before he ran for president. We need Trump to make America laugh again.

Write an essay in which you explain how Obeidallah builds an argument to persuade his audience that Trump's inability to take a joke is worthy of concern. In your essay, analyze how Obeidallah uses one or more of the features listed above (or features of your own choice) to strengthen the logic and persuasiveness of his argument. Be sure that your analysis focuses on the most relevant features of the passage.

Your essay should not explain whether you agree with Obeidallah's claims, but rather explain how the author builds an argument to persuade his audience.

Pre-Essay Writing

Read the essay prompt before you read the provided text. Make sure you have a firm grasp on what the prompt is asking you to analyze in your essay. In this case, the prompt specifically says, "explain how Obeidallah builds an argument to persuade his audience that Trump's inability to take a joke is worthy of concern". A keyword here is "how". How does Obeidallah persuade his audience? Recall the bullet points already given to you, asking you to notice evidence such as facts, statistics, or reliable experience, reasoning that connects ideas through logic and explanation, and stylistic or persuasive elements such as word choice, emotional appeal, building credibility, etc. Obeidallah's techniques will show up in his body paragraphs. As you read, take note of Obeidallah's use of these things and begin to mentally map out your essay.

Some examples from Obeidallah's text:

Facts

a) "In fact, Egypt's Jon Stewart, Bassem Youssef, was arrested for mocking the then leader of Egypt and his TV show was ultimately canceled."

b) "When Seth Meyers skewered Trump at the 2011 White House Correspondent's Dinner, Trump called Meyers "a stutterer."

c) "In the case of Stewart, who for years called out Trump for his outlandish behavior and comments, Trump tweeted that Stewart was "highly overrated" and a "total phony."

d) "And in the case of Maher, Trump actually sued the comedian for $5 million."

Reasoning

a) "I can't recall any President or presidential nominee responding to a TV show mocking him or her by saying it's time to take that show off the airwaves."

b) "Although I have performed stand-up in the Middle East, where leaders have shared a similar sentiment."

c) "Couple all this with Trump's calls during this campaign to change the libel laws to make it easier for him to sue media outlets who unfairly criticize him, and this is no laughing matter."

d) "Comedians, fearing both his social media presence and the wrath of the millions of his Twitter followers, could remain silent on all Trump-related matters."

Stylistic Elements

a) **Fragments:** "But there was Trump, just 24 days before the election, composing yet another unhinged tweet as most Americans were still sleeping," "And in the case of Maher, Trump actually sued the comedian for $5 million," "And even if Trump never went that far, his attacks on "SNL" could have a chilling effect," etc.

b) **Strong word choice:** "unhinged," "skewering," "chilling," "wrath," etc.

c) **Clear transitions:** "Now," "All kidding aside," "In the case of Stewart," etc.

Persuasive Elements

a) **Comparisons:** "In fact, Egypt's Jon Stewart, Bassem Youssef, was arrested for mocking the then leader of Egypt and his TV show was ultimately canceled. But is that really a model we want to emulate in the United States?" Etc.

b) **Credibility:** "Although I have performed stand-up in the Middle East, where leaders have shared a similar sentiment." Etc.

c) **Rhetorical questions:** "But is that really a model we want to emulate in the United States?" "Would a President Trump use the apparatus of the federal government -- such as the Federal Communications Commission -- to intimidate comedians and dissuade them from mocking him?" Etc.

Thoroughly read through the entire text given, paying special attention to key points. You will only have time for one full read through. Key points will be quickly exposed through a thesis-like statement and topic sentences. An author's thesis statement most often appears in the introductory paragraph and sometimes title. Obeidallah's thesis is implied in the title and throughout his essay.

Obeidallah's Thesis:

All kidding aside, Trump's tweet that "SNL" needs to be canceled because the show did a "hit job" on him should concern every American.

Obeidallah's Topic sentences:

Topic sentences are the first sentence of every paragraph.

"Nothing says Donald Trump has the judgment and temperament to be President of the United States like tweeting at 7:14 on Sunday morning that he thinks "Saturday Night Live" should be canceled."

"Apparently Trump was upset with the way SNL depicted him in a sketch based on the second presidential debate."

"All kidding aside, Trump's tweet that "SNL" needs to be canceled because the show did a "hit job" on him should concern every American."

"Although I have performed stand-up in the Middle East, where leaders have shared a similar sentiment."

Etc.

The author's key points will be the structure that your own key points mimic. In this case, Obeidallah's key points are Trumps repeated angry reactions, how these reactions differ from others', and how readers should interpret these reactions. Analyze these points for persuasive techniques, and you have examples, comparisons, and rhetorical questions. These three things are the "how" that the sample essay chooses to focus on, but Obeidallah uses other techniques (like those examples given above), as well, to persuade his audience. No two essays will be alike as you and your peers will analyze Obeidallah's work through a personal lens.

Create a clear and concise thesis that states the author's persuasive techniques.

Sample essay's thesis: *He supports this claim by recalling many examples, making comparisons to Trump's actions, and using rhetorical questions.*

For detailed analysis, these techniques could reasonably be a list of 2-4 (3, in the sample essay's case). One essay style is to focus each body paragraph on one of those techniques. Another style would be to summarize like techniques in paragraphs together. Paraphrase and quote a few specific lines from the text that support your analysis. Keep any quotes used relatively short. Make sure to always surround a quote with your own words. Introduce the quote, include the quote, and then clearly explain why this quote shows the author's persuasive technique. The essay should be mostly your words, not the authors.

Conclude your essay by pointing out the author's intentions, along with their specific audience. Avoid merely restating your thesis.

Sample essay: *If Trump were to become president, he would be open to a lot of criticism, and Obeidallah is concerned about Trump's ability to take jokes. Obeidallah appeals to the American people, arguing that it is an attribute worthy of worry. Trump has a pattern of thin skin, doesn't reach par of past presidential demeanor, and hopefully, American voters can recognize all of this with their own eyes.*

14

Answer Sheet

Use a No. 2 pencil. Begin your essay on this page. If you need more space, continue on the next page.

14

Sample Essay

Donald Trump has an active presence on Twitter. As he becomes more active in the 2016 presidential election his Tweets undergo deep scrutiny, and to one citizen, these tweets are a source of concern. Dean Obeidallah argues that American citizens should be worried about Donald Trump's inability to take a joke. He supports this claim by recalling recorded evidence, making comparisons to Trump's actions, and using rhetorical questions.

Obeidallah shows his audience that there is no lack of recorded evidence when it comes to Trump and his harsh reactions. The article goes through example after example of negative tweets and actions taken against comedians who targeted Trump. Obeidallah recalls how Trump suggested cancelling SNL, called Seth Meyers "a stutterer," called Jon Stewart "a total phony," sued Bill Maher, and attempted to change libel laws. Obeidallah's litany of examples aim to show the reader that Trump's emotional reaction to satire was not a one-off, and one would expect thicker skin in a presidential nominee. The long list of Trump's interactions with comedians, shown in such few words, also helps the reader feel the embarrassment of Trump's rash reactions mounting on top of each other.

Obeidallah drives his argument further by taking Trump's reactions to satirical jokes and comparing them to how others in political positions react. Obeidallah makes his first comparison when he states, "We have a rich tradition of comedy shows skewering our politicians," and with that tradition, past presidential nominees have never threatened cancelling the show. Obeidallah aims to show Americans that Trumps behavior is not an acceptable behavior frequently adopted by those in power. In fact, in one particular SNL sketch, Trump and Hillary Clinton were both criticized, but Hillary never reacted negatively. Obeidallah points out that, here, Hillary has better professional demeanor. Perhaps the most embarrassing comparison Obeidallah makes is Trump to Middle Eastern leaders. He recalls a time when Bassem Youssef was arrested and his show canceled because he poked fun at an Egyptian leader. Trump encouraging the cancellation of SNL is a similar situation. Obeidallah brings up these parallels to show readers that harsh Middle Eastern practices are not the practices we want American leaders implementing.

Lastly, Obeidallah uses rhetorical questions in an effort to get his readers to recognize the flaws in Trump's actions. When referring to the Trump/Middle Eastern comparison, Obeidallah asks, "But is that really a model we want to emulate in the United States?" Instead of making a statement, Obeidallah asks the question in hopes that the readers realize the answer is a resounding "no". He knows that a reader's realization is stronger than his own suggestion. Then, Obeidallah recalls Trump's many attempts to change libel laws for his own campaign and monetary advantage. He asks, "Would a President Trump use the apparatus of the federal government - such as the Federal Communications Commission -- to intimidate comedians and dissuade them from mocking him?" After explaining Trump's pattern of attacking comedian and satirical institutions, Obeidallah implies that the answer to this question should be a resounding "yes". Both rhetorical questions have answers with scary outcomes; Obeidallah aims to help the American people realize this scary outcome could be our future.

If Trump were to become president, he would be open to a lot of criticism, and Obeidallah is concerned about Trump's ability to take jokes. Obeidallah appeals to the American people, arguing that it is an attribute worthy of worry. Trump has a pattern of thin skin, doesn't reach par of past presidential demeanor, and hopefully, American voters can recognize all of this with their own eyes.

Essay 15

Prompt

As you read the passage below, consider how Steinhauer uses

- ❏ evidence, such as facts or examples, to support claims.

- ❏ reasoning to develop ideas and to connect claims and evidence.

- ❏ stylistic or persuasive elements, such as word choice or appeals to emotion, to add power to the ideas expressed.

Adapted from Jason Steinhauer, "The Twitter problem that could change history" ©2017 by CNN. Originally published July 02, 2017.

1. Those distracted by our recent political theater may have missed an extraordinary international incident at the end of May: Russia and Ukraine got into a Twitter war about history.

2. A brief recap of what occurred: Russian President Vladimir Putin held a press conference with French President Emmanuel Macron in France. During the briefing, Putin proudly stated that the wife of French medieval King Henry I, Anna Yaroslavna, was Russian.

3. A Ukrainian Twitter account tweeted that, in fact, Yaroslavna was from Kiev, not Russia.

4. The official Twitter account for Russia tweeted back: "We are proud of our common history ... (we) share the same historical heritage which should unite our nations, not divide us."

5. To which Ukraine tweeted this GIF from "The Simpsons." [A UN representative with a revolving Soviet Union and Russia nametag]

6. The exchange garnered thousands of reactions on Twitter, ranging from laughter and shock to citizen historians sharing their own interpretations of what the medieval Slavic states looked like.

7. Absent from the conversation? The voices of historians, who are critical in providing honest assessments based on well-researched evidence.

8. Hundreds of millions of people now consume historical information on social media, either directly or via links. According to a 2016 Pew survey, a majority of US adults - 62% - get news on social media, and 18% do so often. The same study found that nearly 6-in-10 Twitter users get news on Twitter. Few go to academic monographs or journal articles to dig deeper.

9. A forum such as Twitter is therefore an important opportunity to clarify information for citizens and hold

15

political leaders and state actors accountable in their use and abuse of the past.

10. Often on Twitter many of the comments and responses rely on facts from Wikipedia or other sources that may not be thoroughly researched. Additionally, many of the replies (including those from the two nations involved) are politically motivated and as such may not be trustworthy or objective. This is where historians play an important role in setting the record straight.

11. Of course, the issue of historical accuracy isn't a uniquely Russia-Ukraine story. On behalf of the US State Department, I was recently in Lithuania, where Russian media are asserting that since Soviet troops won the land of Lithuania during World War II, it should now be returned to Russia. This is part of a larger effort by Russian media and military to discredit Lithuanian history and justify a return to a Soviet-style sphere of influence.

12. That's where we need the voices of historians to cut through the clutter. Indeed, this was my message in meeting with US and Lithuanian officials in addition to scholars and students. It is why a group of historians; media scholars and science communicators nationwide have established the field of "history communication" to train historians to be media-savvy and to empower them to use new media to promote their scholarship.

13. Historians have taken great steps to get out of the classroom and into cyberspace. Dozens of historians are working together on a new history blog for The Washington Post, and there are several history-themed podcasts and websites publishing historical scholarship.

14. But we need to go even further.

15. Many historians, including those who work on Russia, have Twitter accounts. My list of historians on Twitter is now more than 1,100 members. Some historians, such as Kevin Kruse, Joanne Freeman and Heather Cox Richardson, are already taking it upon themselves to interject their expertise into contested exchanges about the past. It cannot stop with them.

16. The subtext for the Russia-Ukraine exchange is complex. And it's part of a larger Russian effort to establish legitimate claims to former Soviet lands through influencing public opinion.

17. History, of course, plays an important role in this process. Before Moscow annexed Crimea, it set out to establish Russia's historic ties to the peninsula and rallied support among the residents for a return to their Russian homeland.

18. Whereas in the past these contestations over history may have played out in books, the mainstream media and academia, today they also occur over the Internet and social media.

19. We need historians to be there at the ready to disentangle myth from fact.

Write an essay in which you explain how Steinhauer builds an argument to persuade his audience that historians need a larger presence on Twitter. In your essay, analyze how Steinhauer uses one or more of the features listed above (or features of your own choice) to strengthen the logic and persuasiveness of his argument. Be sure that your analysis focuses on the most relevant features of the passage.

Your essay should not explain whether you agree with Steinhauer's claims, but rather explain how the author builds an argument to persuade his audience.

Pre-Essay Writing

Read the essay prompt before you read the provided text. Make sure you have a firm grasp on what the prompt is asking you to analyze in your essay. In this case, the prompt specifically says, "explain how Steinhauer builds an argument to persuade his audience that historians need a larger presence on Twitter". A keyword here is "how". How does Steinhauer persuade his audience? Recall the bullet points already given to you, asking you to notice evidence such as facts, statistics, or reliable experience, reasoning that connects ideas through logic and explanation, and stylistic or persuasive elements such as word choice, emotional appeal, building credibility, etc. Steinhauer's techniques will show up in his body paragraphs. As you read, take note of Steinhauer's use of these things and begin to mentally map out your essay.

Some examples from Steinhauer's text:

Facts

a) "During the briefing, Putin proudly stated that the wife of French medieval King Henry I, Anna Yaroslavna, was Russian."

b) "A Ukrainian Twitter account tweeted that, in fact, Yaroslavna was from Kiev, not Russia."

c) "The exchange garnered thousands of reactions on Twitter, ranging from laughter and shock to citizen historians sharing their own interpretations of what the medieval Slavic states looked like."

d) "On behalf of the US State Department, I was recently in Lithuania, where Russian media are asserting that since Soviet troops won the land of Lithuania during World War II, it should now be returned to Russia."

Statistics

a) "According to a 2016 Pew survey, a majority of US adults - 62%

b) "get news on social media, and 18% do so often."

15

c) "The same study found that nearly 6-in-10 Twitter users get news on Twitter."

d) "My list of historians on Twitter is now more than 1,100 members."

Reasoning

a) "A forum such as Twitter is therefore an important opportunity to clarify information for citizens and hold political leaders and state actors accountable in their use and abuse of the past."

b) "Additionally, many of the replies (including those from the two nations involved) are politically motivated and as such may not be trustworthy or objective."

c) "Of course, the issue of historical accuracy isn't a uniquely Russia-Ukraine story."

d) "It is why a group of historians; media scholars and science communicators nationwide have established the field of "history communication" to train historians to be media-savvy and to empower them to use new media to promote their scholarship."

Stylistic Elements

a) **Clear transitions:** "therefore," "additionally," "of course," "indeed," etc.

b) **Repetition:** "This is where historians play an important role in setting the record straight." "The voices of historians, who are critical in providing honest assessments based on well-researched evidence." "That's where we need the voices of historians to cut through the clutter." Etc.

c) **Compare past to present:** "Few go to academic monographs or journal articles to dig deeper." "Historians have taken great steps to get out of the classroom and into cyberspace." "Whereas in the past these contestations over history may have played out in books, the mainstream media and academia, today they also occur over the Internet and social media" Etc.

Persuasive Elements

a) **Strong phrasing:** "use and abuse," "politically motivated," "cut through the clutter," "history communication," "disentangle myth from fact," etc.

b) **Trustworthy/Objective:** "Often on Twitter..." "may not be thoroughly researched," etc.

c) **Credibility:** "Dozens of historians are working together on a new history blog for The Washington Post, and there are several history-themed podcasts and websites publishing historical scholarship." "Some historians, such as Kevin Kruse, Joanne Freeman and Heather Cox Richardson, are already taking it upon themselves to interject their expertise into contested exchanges about the past." Etc.

15 Thoroughly read through the entire text given, paying special attention to key points. You will only have time for one full read through. Key points will be quickly exposed through a thesis-like statement and topic sentences. An author's thesis statement most often appears in the introductory paragraph. Steinhauer's thesis appears after a bit of background.

Steinhauer's Thesis:

Absent from the conversation? The voices of historians, who are critical in providing honest assessments based on well-researched evidence.

Steinhauer's Topic sentences:

Topic sentences are the first sentence of every paragraph.

"Those distracted by our recent political theater may have missed an extraordinary international incident at the end of May: Russia and Ukraine got into a Twitter war about history."

"The exchange garnered thousands of reactions on Twitter, ranging from laughter and shock to citizen historians sharing their own interpretations of what the medieval Slavic states looked like."

"Hundreds of millions of people now consume historical information on social media, either directly or via links."

"Of course, the issue of historical accuracy isn't a uniquely Russia-Ukraine story."

Etc.

The author's key points will be the structure that your own key points mimic. In this case, Steinhauer's key points are Russian fact manipulation, a rise in social media reliance, and a need to teach correct history. Analyze these points for persuasive techniques, and you have recent examples, statistics, and strong phrasing. These three things are the "how" that the sample essay chooses to focus on, but Steinhauer uses other techniques (like those examples given above), as well, to persuade his audience. No two essays will be alike as you and your peers will analyze Steinhauer's work through a personal lens.

Create a clear and concise thesis that states the author's persuasive techniques.

Sample essay's thesis: *He supports his claim by using recent examples, statistics, and strong phrasing.*

For detailed analysis, these techniques could reasonably be a list of 2-4 (3, in the sample essay's case). One essay style is to focus each body paragraph on one of those techniques. Another style would be to summarize like techniques in paragraphs together. Paraphrase and quote a few specific lines from the text that support your analysis. Keep any quotes used relatively short. Make sure to always surround a quote with your own words. Introduce the quote, include the quote, and then clearly explain why this quote shows the author's persuasive technique. The essay should be mostly your words, not the authors.

Conclude your essay by pointing out the author's intentions, along with their specific audience. Avoid merely restating your thesis.

Sample essay: *Steinhauer speaks to a niche audience, but his message is clear. Social media can be a great source of information, but only if the right information is spread. If you're a person who knows a lot about history, create a presence on Twitter and speak up, if you're not, let the historians do the work.*

15

Answer Sheet

Use a No. 2 pencil. Begin your essay on this page. If you need more space, continue on the next page.

Sample Essay

It seems society is turning to social media for everything these days, including news and facts from history. It is a convenient place to get information, but you can't believe everything you read on the internet. In his article for CNN, Jason Steinhauer pleads with historians, arguing that they need to have a much larger presence on Twitter in order to set records straight. He supports his claim by using recent examples, statistics, and strong phrasing.

Steinhauer calls upon recent confusion to give historians an example of why they're needed. He recounts a disagreement between Russia and Ukraine that started when Vladimir Putin claimed that Anna Yaroslavna was Russian. In a public fashion, Ukraine used their Twitter account to correct Putin, stating that she was from Kiev. Steinhauer points out that while the conversation only lasted a few more exchanges, reactions of "laughter and shock" by other Twitter users were abundant. It was the historians who were absent. The Russia/Ukraine disagreement shows Steinhauer's historians how quickly incorrect information could be pushed out, and how quickly incorrect information could be passed on. He mentions that those trying to correct the problem may be uninformed, turning to unreliable sources like Wikipedia. It should be clear that a historian would be a much better source here. Similarly, Steinhauer gives an example where Russian media was manipulating the history of Lithuania, claiming that it should be Russian land since they won it in WWII. Steinhauer's examples show listening historians that an easy fix to the spread of misinformation is their knowledgeable voice in the media.

More than just two recent examples, Steinhauer relays statistics that display the use of social media for information. It appears print text is becoming a thing of the past as Steinhauer quotes a 2016 Pew Survey as saying, "a majority of US adults - 62% - get news on social media, and 18% do so often. The same study found that nearly 6-in-10 Twitter users get news on Twitter". Steinhauer uses this statistic to show the staggering number of adults that could be receiving incorrect information as it quickly spreads across the internet without a fact-checking historian. A specific statistic about adults also makes the reader wonder if statistics about children would be even higher. Given the reliance on social media, there are some historians who are making their presence known on Twitter. Steinhauer has a list of 1,100 historians on Twitter so far. He uses this number to show that, while there's a start, there aren't enough people combing the thousands upon thousands of retweeted bits of information every day. It's a start, he says, but "it cannot stop with them". Every reading historian needs to play a part.

Lastly, Steinhauer uses strong phrasing to reinforce the need for reliable sources on social media. He calls the Russia/Ukraine debate an "extraordinary international incident". This bold label aims to put more pressure on the outcome of such an event, so the reader will take it more seriously. Steinhauer continues with his bold choices when he claims that there is a "use and abuse of the past" when politicians spin history for their own agendas. This image of abuse creates a bit of guilt in the historian audience, urging them to feel accountable in stopping fact manipulation. Steinhauer achieves this guilt again when he says historians are needed to "cut through the clutter" or "disentangle myth from fact". These strong phrases create images of the reader playing a major role in helping society sort fact from fiction, a fulfilling image for someone so in love with history.

Steinhauer speaks to a niche audience, but his message is clear. Social media can be a great source of information, but only if the right information is spread. If you're a person who knows a lot about history, create a presence on Twitter and speak up, if you're not, let the historians do the work.

Essay 16

Prompt

As you read the passage below, consider how Shaw uses

❑ evidence, such as facts or examples, to support claims.

❑ reasoning to develop ideas and to connect claims and evidence.

❑ stylistic or persuasive elements, such as word choice or appeals to emotion, to add power to the ideas expressed.

Adapted from Rebecca Shaw, "Colleen McCullough: we'll celebrate a woman for anything, as long as it's not her talent" ©2017 by The Guardian. Originally published January 29, 2015.

1. Obituaries are a funny thing. How do you sum up a person's entire life in just a few words? How do you put their essence on a page, touching on their achievements, and their greatest moments, while also keeping it personal? The first paragraph seems to be crucial. When Bryce Courtenay, one of Australia's most beloved and successful authors died in 2012, the Australian newspaper started out with:

2. BRYCE Courtenay was one of Australia's greatest storytellers, touching the hearts of millions of people around the world with 21 bestselling books including The Power of One.

3. Lovely. In this introduction you understand immediately that he was a best-selling author, a great story-teller, and someone who touched the lives of many people through his work. Seems easy enough. Yesterday, the Australian published an obituary for another beloved and best-selling Australian author, Colleen McCullough. Her obituary opened with:

4. COLLEEN McCullough, Australia's best-selling author, was a charmer. Plain of feature, and certainly over-weight, she was, nevertheless, a woman of wit and warmth. In one interview, she said: "I've never been into clothes or figure and the interesting thing is I never had any trouble attracting men."

5. Now, what do we learn from this introduction? The fact that she was a best-selling author is quickly tossed aside in order to discuss her looks and her success with men. In the first paragraph. Of her obituary. Which is meant to sum up her entire life. McCullough was a woman who penned The Thorn Birds, still the high-est-selling Australian book of all time. After working as a neuroscientist in Sydney, she went on to write that particular book during her time in the neurology department at Yale. This is a woman who also wrote an acclaimed seven-book, methodically researched, historical series called Masters of Rome, which won her diverse fans like Newt Gingrich and Bob Carr. She is someone who accomplished an astonishing amount during her life, and here she is reduced, in a moment, to her looks and her ability to attract men.

16

6.	Sadly, this is not an issue that is restricted to this particular newspaper (although it is a clear and awful example of it), or to McCullough herself. When the accomplished and brilliant rocket scientist Yvonne Brill passed away in 2013, the New York Times came under fire for their obituary, which began with:

7.	She made a mean beef stroganoff, followed her husband from job to job and took eight years off from work to raise three children. "The world's best mom," her son Matthew said.

8.	But Yvonne Brill, who died on Wednesday at 88 in Princeton, N.J., was also a brilliant rocket scientist, who in the early 1970s invented a propulsion system to help keep communications satellites from slipping out of their orbits.

9.	Once again, a woman's life full of incredible accomplishments. Once again, a woman reduced to her position in relation to men, and this time, how good her cooking is.

10.	That these outrageous obituaries still being published demonstrates how little has changed, and how women's lives are still too often abridged and disrespected. It shows us where the emphasis remains; a woman's physical attractiveness and relationships with men are given more weight than her personal accomplishments.

11.	"BUT" Brill was also a brilliant rocket scientist, even though she was a woman and a mother. As if the two are mutually exclusive. Yes, Colleen McCullough was plain and overweight, "NEVERTHELESS" she was warm and had wit and could attract men. As if those attributes are mutually exclusive. As if that is an important thing to note at all, let alone in the first paragraph of her obituary. The summation of their lives; centered around men.

12.	Personal relationships, husbands, wives and children are no doubt vitally important in many people's lives and should be discussed when looking back. But all too often women are firstly classed and summed up by their roles as wives and mothers, rather than by their other accomplishments. The life of a brilliant male scientist would never immediately be reduced to his looks, or how many wives he had. He would be remembered first for his accomplishments. In the pages of these major publications, women deserve the same.

Write an essay in which you explain how Shaw builds an argument to persuade her audience that women need to be recognized for their accomplishments, first. In your essay, analyze how Shaw uses one or more of the features listed above (or features of your own choice) to strengthen the logic and persuasiveness of her argument. Be sure that your analysis focuses on the most relevant features of the passage.

Your essay should not explain whether you agree with Shaw's claims, but rather explain how the author builds an argument to persuade her audience.

Pre-Essay Writing

Read the essay prompt before you read the provided text. Make sure you have a firm grasp on what the prompt is asking you to analyze in your essay. In this case, the prompt specifically says, "explain how Shaw builds an argument to persuade her audience that women need to be recognized for their accomplishments, first.". A keyword here is "how". How does Shaw persuade her audience? Recall the bullet points already given to you, asking you to notice evidence such as facts, statistics, or reliable experience, reasoning that connects ideas through logic and explanation, and stylistic or persuasive elements such as word choice, emotional appeal, building credibility, etc. Shaw's techniques will show up in her body paragraphs. As you read, take note of Shaw's use of these things and begin to mentally map out your essay.

Some examples from Shaw's text:

Facts

a) "When Bryce Courtenay, one of Australia's most beloved and successful authors died in 2012, the Australian newspaper started out with…"

b) "Yesterday, the Australian published an obituary for another beloved and best-selling Australian author, Colleen McCullough."

c) "McCullough was a woman who penned The Thorn Birds, still the highest-selling Australian book of all time."

d) "When the accomplished and brilliant rocket scientist Yvonne Brill passed away in 2013, the New York Times came under fire for their obituary, which began with…"

Reasoning

a) "In this introduction you understand immediately that he was a best-selling author, a great storyteller, and someone who touched the lives of many people through his work. Seems easy enough."

16

b) "Now, what do we learn from this introduction? The fact that she was a best-selling author is quickly tossed aside in order to discuss her looks and her success with men."

c) "It shows us where the emphasis remains; a woman's physical attractiveness and relationships with men are given more weight than her personal accomplishments."

d) "The life of a brilliant male scientist would never immediately be reduced to his looks, or how many wives he had."

Stylistic Elements

a) Rhetorical questions: "How do you sum up a person's entire life in just a few words? How do you put their essence on a page, touching on their achievements, and their greatest moments, while also keeping it personal?" "Now, what do we learn from this introduction?"

b) Fragments: "Lovely." "In the first paragraph. Of her obituary. Which is meant to sum up her entire life." "Once again, a woman's life full of incredible accomplishments." etc.

c) Repetition: "Once again, a woman's life full of incredible accomplishments. Once again, a woman reduced to her position in relation to men, and this time, how good her cooking is." "As if those attributes are mutually exclusive. As if that is an important thing to note at all, let alone in the first paragraph of her obituary." etc.

Persuasive Elements

a) Emotional appeal: "BUT" Brill was also a brilliant rocket scientist, even though she was a woman and a mother. As if the two are mutually exclusive. Yes, Colleen McCullough was plain and overweight, "NEVERTHELESS" she was warm and had wit and could attract men. As if those attributes are mutually exclusive. As if that is an important thing to note at all, let alone in the first paragraph of her obituary. The summation of their lives; centered around men."

b) Angry word choice: "tossed aside," "reduced," "outrageous," etc.

c) Credibility: The Australian, The New York Times

Thoroughly read through the entire text given, paying special attention to key points. You will only have time for one full read through. Key points will be quickly exposed through a thesis-like statement and topic sentences. An author's thesis statement most often appears in the introductory paragraph or can be hinted at in the title. In Shaw's case, her clear thesis appears at the end of the article but is implied in the title and throughout the text.

Shaw's Thesis:

But all too often women are firstly classed and summed up by their roles as wives and mothers, rather than by their other accomplishments.

Shaw's Topic sentences:

Topic sentences are the first sentence of every paragraph.

"Obituaries are a funny thing."

"Now, what do we learn from this introduction? The fact that she was a best-selling author is quickly tossed aside in order to discuss her looks and her success with men."

"Sadly, this is not an issue that is restricted to this particular newspaper (although it is a clear and awful example of it), or to McCullough herself."

"That these outrageous obituaries still being published demonstrates how little has changed, and how women's lives are still too often abridged and disrespected."

Etc.

The author's key points will be the structure that your own key points mimic. In this case, Shaw's key points are the different wording of male and female obituaries, what this wording suggests about men and women, and the subsequent change that needs to be taken when describing women. Analyze these points for persuasive techniques, and you have compare/contrast, fragments, and angry word choice. These three things are the "how" that the sample essay chooses to focus on, but Shaw uses other techniques (like those examples given above), as well, to persuade her audience. No two essays will be alike as you and your peers will analyze Shaw's work through a personal lens.

Create a clear and concise thesis that states the author's persuasive techniques.

Sample essay's thesis: *She supports her claim by using the stylistic elements of compare/contrast, fragments, and angry word choice.*

For detailed analysis, these techniques could reasonably be a list of 2-4 (3, in the sample essay's case). One essay style is to focus each body paragraph on one of those techniques. Another style would be to summarize like techniques in paragraphs together. Paraphrase and quote a few specific lines from the text that support your analysis. Keep any quotes used relatively short. Make sure to always surround a quote with your own words. Introduce the quote, include the quote, and then clearly explain why this quote shows the author's persuasive technique. The essay should be mostly your words, not the authors.

Conclude your essay by pointing out the author's intentions, along with their specific audience. Avoid merely restating your thesis.

Sample essay: *Whether Shaw's audience is writers, getting them to improve the written image of women, or Shaw's audience is everyone, getting them to put women and men on the same plane of importance, her article shows that a clear disparity between genders does exist. Women can be accomplished. Remember women for those accomplishments, first.*

16

Answer Sheet

Use a No. 2 pencil. Begin your essay on this page. If you need more space, continue on the next page.

Sample Essay

Obituaries are mere snapshots into the lives of those we've lost. For that reason, it's rare that in so few words we can do any justice honoring the lives of those who've passed. According to Rebecca Shaw, it's even more rare to truly honor the lives of women. In her article for The Guardian, she argues that women need to be recognized for their accomplishments first, above all else. She supports her claim by using the stylistic elements of compare/contrast, fragments, and angry word choice.

Not all obituaries are created equal. To prove this point, Shaw compares the structure of two obituaries for famous authors, one male and one female, in the Australian newspaper. Bryce Courtenay's, the male's, starts immediately by explaining his famed storytelling and the large impact it has had on readers. Colleen McCullough's, the female's, starts immediately by calling her a "charmer". The two following sentences describe McCullough's "plain" features, "overweight" body, and wit. Shaw juxtaposes these two obituaries to clearly show the reader that there's an unfair disparity. You might not even realize that McCullough was a best-selling author and neuroscientist, if Shaw didn't go on to list McCullough's real accomplishments. Shaw's comparison also pushes the audience to ask why the two obituaries are different, if both Courtenay and McCullough were famous, beloved, Australian authors. Just in case the cause isn't clear, Shaw gives another example to add to the comparison. Yvonne Brill was a rocket scientist, but the New York Times first memorialized her for excellent beef stroganoff, a husband, and three kids. Shaw gives this third comparison to show that the difference is, indeed, gender, and Courtenay and McCullough's obituaries were not standalone instances.

Shaw continues to create pause about obituary gender inequality by using fragments in her writing. A fragment, in Shaw's case, is not a grammar mistake, but an opportunity to add emphasis to her message. After explaining to the reader that McCullough's accomplishments have been ignored, Shaw states, "In the first paragraph. Of her obituary. Which is meant to sum up her entire life." These fragments cause the reader to think about the offensive nature of this move, pausing at each pointed detail. Shaw does this again after sampling from Brill's obituary. She writes, "Once again, a woman's life full of incredible accomplishments. Once again, a woman reduced to her position in relation to men, and this time, how good her cooking is." These incomplete sentences are basic thoughts that interpret the basic mistake of these women's obituaries. Shaw urges writers and readers to pause and notice.

It's clear that Shaw is passionate about this subject, so she employs specific word choice in her writing to incite similar anger in her audience. In describing McCullough's obituary, Shaw says the important details of her life are "tossed aside". This phrase aims to get the reader to imagine McCullough's impressive accomplishments being thrown into a trash heap, an infuriating image. Shaw uses the word "reduced" three times, twice in correlation with how McCullough and Brill are portrayed in their obituaries, and once attached to a male for comparison. "Reduced" connotes a smaller presence of these women in death, than in life, invalidated and underappreciated. If you would n't reduce a male, don't reduce a woman. In a final burst of passion, Shaw states, "That these outrageous obituaries still being published demonstrates how little has changed, and how women's lives are still too often abridged and disrespected." "Outrageous", "abridged", and "disrespected" are all negative words that Shaw hopes to associate with obituaries that don't do the incredible lives of women any justice.

Whether Shaw's audience is writers, getting them to improve the written image of women, or Shaw's audience is everyone, getting them to put women and men on the same plane of importance, her article shows that a clear disparity between genders does exist. Women can be accomplished. Remember women for those accomplishments, first.

16

CPSIA information can be obtained
at www.ICGtesting.com
Printed in the USA
LVHW012354250121
677443LV00011B/1238

9 781949 395624